BLACK DOG, BLACK NIGHT

ALSO BY PAUL HOOVER

Books

Edge and Fold (poetry), Berkeley: Apogee Press, 2006.
Poems in Spanish (poetry), Albany, CA: Omnidawn Press, 2005.
Fables of Representation (essays), Ann Arbor:
University of Michigan Press, 2004.
Winter (Mirror) (poetry), Chicago: Flood Editions, 2002.
Rehearsal in Black (poetry), Cambridge, England: Salt Publications, 2001.
Totem and Shadow: New & Selected Poems,
Jersey City: Talisman House, 1999.
Viridian (poetry), Athens, GA: University of Georgia Press, 1997.
The Novel: A Poem, New York: New Directions, 1990.
Saigon, Illinois (novel), New York: Vintage Contemporaries, 1988.
Idea (poetry), Great Barrington, MA: The Figures, 1987.
Nervous Songs (poetry), Seattle: L'Epervier Press, 1986.
Somebody Talks a Lot (poetry), Chicago: The Yellow Press, 1983.
Letter to Einstein Beginning Dear Albert (poetry),
Chicago: The Yellow Press, 1979.

Publications Edited

Postmodern American Poetry: A Norton Anthology,
New York: W. W. Norton, 1994.
New American Writing (literary magazine),
Chicago: OINK! Press, 1987 to present.

Translations

33 Poems of Nguyen Trai, edited and translated with
Nguyen Do. Ho Chi Minh City: Saigon Culture.
Selected Poems of Friedrich Hölderlin, edited and translated
with Maxine Chernoff.

BLACK DOG, BLACK NIGHT

CONTEMPORARY VIETNAMESE POETRY

....

EDITED AND TRANSLATED BY

Nguyen Do and Paul Hoover

MILKWEED EDITIONS

Published 2008 by Milkweed Editions
Printed in Canada
Cover design by Christian Fünfhausen
Cover art, "Between the Lines," by Thien Do
Interior design by Wendy Holdman, BookMobile Design & Publishing·Services
The text of this book is set in Minion Pro.
08 09 10 11 12   5 4 3 2 1
First Edition

Milkweed Editions, a nonprofit publisher, gratefully acknowledges sustaining support from Anonymous; Emilie and Henry Buchwald; the Bush Foundation; the Patrick and Aimee Butler Family Foundation; CarVal Investors; the Dougherty Family Foundation; the Ecolab Foundation; the General Mills Foundation; the Claire Giannini Fund; John and Joanne Gordon; William and Jeanne Grandy; the Jerome Foundation; Dorothy Kaplan Light and Ernest Light; Constance B. Kunin; Marshall BankFirst Corp.; Sanders and Tasha Marvin; the May Department Stores Company Foundation; the McKnight Foundation; a grant from the Minnesota State Arts Board, through an appropriation by the Minnesota State Legislature, a grant from the National Endowment for the Arts, and private funders; an award from the National Endowment for the Arts, which believes that a great nation deserves great art; the Navarre Corporation; Debbie Reynolds; the Starbucks Foundation; the St. Paul Travelers Foundation; Ellen and Sheldon Sturgis; the Target Foundation; the Gertrude Sexton Thompson Charitable Trust (George R. A. Johnson, Trustee); the James R. Thorpe Foundation; the Toro Foundation; Moira and John Turner; United Parcel Service; Joanne and Phil Von Blon; Kathleen and Bill Wanner; Serene and Christopher Warren; the W. M. Foundation; and the Xcel Energy Foundation.

Library of Congress Cataloging-in-Publication Data

Black dog, black night : contemporary Vietnamese poetry / edited and translated by Nguyen Do and Paul Hoover. — 1st ed.
p. cm.
Includes bibliographical references.
ISBN 978-1-57131-430-7 (pbk. with flaps : alk. paper)
1. Vietnamese poetry—Translations into English. I. Nguyen, Do, 1959- II. Hoover, Paul, 1946–
PL4378.65.E5B53 2008
895.9'221408—dc22   2007042223
                                            CIP

This book is printed on acid-free, recycled (100% postconsumer waste) paper.

MINNESOTA
STATE ARTS BOARD

NATIONAL
ENDOWMENT
FOR THE ARTS

CONTENTS

CONTEMPORARY VIETNAMESE POETRY: INVISIBILITY AND THE NEW HORIZON

Nguyen Do

When I left my country to live in the United States to study English, my fellow poets asked when I would return. I smiled: I would be back, but not until I was able to translate my own poetry and that of other Vietnamese poets into English. Now that possibility—a new horizon—is becoming reality, but not only for me; a new horizon also appears for my cotranslator, the poet Paul Hoover. Not long after I visited him and his wife, poet Maxine Chernoff, in their home, and read his anthology *Postmodern American Poetry*, I also read the controversial diary of Vietnamese poet Tran Dan. These events prompted me to write a poem in English, which I sent to Paul for editing help. The result made me enthusiastic and confident of our ability to work together. Why not make my dream come true by translating Vietnamese poetry into English with Paul, as long as he was willing?

Since the Renovation Movement began in Vietnam in 1989, some Vietnamese poetry has been translated into English. But whose work was being translated, and for what audience? Almost all the poems translated until now were written by government "insiders" such as Pham Tien Duat, Huu Thinh, Nguyen Duy, and Nguyen Quang Thieu who, deemed "veterans," have had the privilege to meet with US authors at the William Joiner Center in Boston, where translation and anthology projects between Vietnam-American War veterans on both sides are encouraged and conceived. Though some of the poets welcomed at the center, including Y Nhi, Nguyen Quang Thieu, and Xuan Quynh, were not veterans, several important Vietnamese poets who *were* veterans, such as Dang Dinh Hung, Van Cao, Tran Dan, Huu Loan, Hoàng Cam, and Thanh Thao, have never been invited. Moreover, many other poets who have produced some of the most important contemporary Vietnamese poetry—new voices and especially new styles—have not yet received any recognition or benefits from the government. These poets—Hoàng Hung, Nguyen Do, and Nhat Le among others—are not veterans, nor are they members of the Vietnamese Writers Association. Barely able to publish in their own country, these "outside" poets have little chance for foreign recognition unless they do the translation work themselves.

In the United States, the concept of the literary outsider is well known, popularized by the Beats. For contemporary Vietnamese "outsider poets," the road is similar but, unfortunately, harsher, with the innovative "outsiders" forced to struggle to survive in a literary landscape dominated by the more traditional "insiders."

Legislated Poetry and Vietnamese Tradition

One day Xuan Dieu (1926-1986), one of the greatest Vietnamese lyric poets, asked a young poet who worked in the Department of Forestry if he knew why Vietnam had been experiencing such great flooding. Not waiting for the answer, Xuan Dieu said, "Because Vietnam has too many poets so they cut too many trees to produce paper for printing poetry. Therefore, its effect is to imbalance nature, causing flooding!" It's not just a joke; it's the reality of Vietnamese poetry and its production.

Poetry has a very important position in Vietnamese tradition. All ceremonies, from funerals to weddings, from folklore festivals to political meetings, begin with poetry. From the factories to the rice fields, from the walls of schools to those of warehouses, everyone can be a poet—soldiers, farmers, the most destitute, and the most powerful national leaders, such as the General Secretary of the Communist Party. In Vietnam, literature (poetry and prose) has its own administrative department comparable to the national legislature, from the national Vietnamese Writers Association down to its branches in cities and provinces and its bureaus of instruction. Poets who work in these bureaus are paid, like any other government officer, according to their rank. Those who do not serve as officers but are members of the Writers Association are subsidized, receive benefits, and have much more opportunity to publish their works than nonmembers. They are also more likely to win many national and local awards. When the government subsidizes poets, the poets may try to produce works consistent with the government's practices and beliefs. Poetry becomes a national chorus of voices singing the same tune. The situation is comparable to Alexander Pope's "The Dunciad":

> In merry old England it once was a rule,
> The King had his Poet, and also his Fool:
> But now we're so frugal, I'd have you to know it,
> That Cibber can serve both for Fool and for Poet

Contemporary Vietnamese poetry is less rigid than it used to be. However, the long-held doctrine of socialist realism in literature still requires that one "pray" rather than "complain" as a writer. Overseen by the poet To Huu (1920-2004), the practice of socialist realism has dominated for more than a half century and is in part responsible for the "insider" dilemma described above. Poets were limited to a uniform structure—a combination of the government's mission and what poets pretended to be their own opinion—and three styles: folk poetry, lyric poetry emerging from nineteenth-century romanticism, and a blend of the two. Before 1989, the system held to two firm rules:

First, in all works of literature, socialists were to always win, never lose. Optimism was required. Poets were to write about life, not death. No criticisms were allowed unless the heads of state wanted them printed. All poems containing these prohibited factors were to be destroyed—for example, Huu Loan's "The Purple Color of Sim Flowers," Quang Dung's "Moving forward to the West," Van

Cao's "Five Unreal Mornings" and "The Garbage Wagon Passing over Da Lac Street," Hoàng Cam's "The Other Side of Duong River" and "Dieu Bong Leaf," and, later in the Vietnam War, Thanh Thao's "A Soldier Speaks of His Generation." Such suppression became especially strong when the Nhan Van ("Humanities") group of writers appeared. Including Tran Dan, Le Dat, Hoàng Cam, Phung Quan, Huu Loan, Dang Dinh Hung, Van Cao, and others, Nhan Van members publicly expressed their alarm at the circumstances of Vietnamese writers. Unfortunately, a ruthless suppression followed, and what began as a great movement toward freedom of speech and the press in Vietnam was destroyed. Writers involved were purged from the Writers Association and imprisoned in "reform camps." Perhaps worst of all, they were forbidden from publishing their work for more than thirty years.

Second, because the government believed that most readers were uneducated farmers who couldn't understand complex expression, poetry had to contain simple rather than complex ideas. Poetry's language and form were thus limited to the traditional and/or lyrically romantic. As a result, Vietnamese poetry became frozen in place. Any poet who broke the rules came under fire, as happened with Nguyen Dinh Thi for a short time in the early 1960s, and later with Hoàng Hung and Dang Dinh Hung.

Some of the "insiders" did choose either to dig deeper into tradition, like Xuan Quynh and Nguyen Duy, or to try to combine that tradition with Western culture, like Te Hanh, Nguyen Khoa Diem, and Nguyen Quang Thieu. In so doing, they have been successful in reaching an audience. Nguyen Duy's work is influenced by Nguyen Binh, a poet of the New Poetry period, 1933-1945, popular for his use of the *luc bat* traditional form of six- and eight-word lines. Xuan Quynh (1942-1988) was the most popular female poet of the contemporary period. Her poetry is an extension of the New Poetry style, which emphasized lyric emotion and form, but she refreshed the style by turning it toward the new circumstances of the Vietnam-American War. Reading the poetry of Te Hanh and Nguyen Khoa Diem is like marching through their souls. Though they are of different generations—the first a leading figure of New Poetry, the other a current political leader comparable to To Huu—both often depart from their own social environments. Their voices are modest, calm, and warm, and they blend Western lyric with the freshness of nature they have observed in central Vietnam. Such poetry has longevity because it relates to the unchanging patterns of everyday life. Te Hanh, Nguyen Khoa Diem, Xuan Quynh, Nguyen Duy, and Y Nhi are among the most popular poets of the Vietnam-American War era.

Poetry of the "Outsiders"

Contemporary Vietnamese poetry began in 1945, when the New Poetry movement, echoing beautifully from French romanticism, came to an end, and Vietnam began its war of resistance to French colonialism. During the period from 1945-1954, Vietnamese poets found their main influence in the Russian poet Vladimir Mayakovsky, as well as what remained of the New Poetry style. Because of Mayakovsky's expansiveness, many poets experimented with longer poems. Examples can be seen in the work of Tran Mai Ninh, Hoàng Trung Thong, Quang Dung, Chinh Huu, and especially the poets of the Nhan Van group, including Huu Loan, Hoàng Cam, Tran Dan, Le Dat, Phung Quan, Van Cao, and Dang Dinh Hung. However, because of the group's suppression by the government, Nhan Van's influence in the renovation of poetry has been felt most strongly in later years. Some Nhan Van poets, like Le Dat and Hoàng Cam, are still alive and writing, and their adherents—with some exceptions, such as unusual word choices and rhymes—continue to write in a style blending the Mayakovsky influence with nineteenth-century French romanticism.

Even though Nhan Van was unable to offer full renovation, it did introduce a new spirit of freedom to poetry and to certain facets of social life. The courageous conduct of Nhan Van and its leader Tran Dan was an inspiration for Dang Dinh Hung, Van Cao, and others; this is the true importance of the Nhan Van achievement.

Although the government was not persuaded to banish censorship completely, after 1989, almost all previously prohibited works were finally published and, later, republished due to liberalization following the collapse of the Soviet Union. Being an "outsider" today indicates that a poet is daring to describe the new, true, and deep emotions of modern life; like Nhan Van, pursuing freedom of expression for writers; and, most significantly, trying to transcend the boundaries of traditional folk lyricism.

The risks inherent in the modern style were apparent in the work of those influenced by Mayakovsky in the French colonial period (1945-1954): Tran Mai Ninh's "Remember Blood" and "Tuy Hoa"; Hong Nguyen's "Remembering"; Huu Loan's "The Ca Pass" and "The Purple Color of Sim Flowers"; Hoàng Cam's "The Other Side of Duong River"; and especially Tran Dan, who has at least four long poems in Mayakovsky's expansive style: "We'll Absolutely Win," "Ho Chi Minh," "Go! Viet Bac," and "The Provincial Gate."

Contemporary Vietnamese poetry took a decidedly new turn when Thanh Thao published *The Rubik's Cube* in 1985, despite the fact that the book was issued by New Works, the official publisher of the Vietnamese Writers Association. This collection struck like a bolt of lightning because, up to that time in Vietnamese history, such a fresh new voice—direct, strong, and hauntingly existential—had never appeared. Influenced by Boris Pasternak (Thanh Thao and his cotranslator were the first to translate Pasternak's work into Vietnamese), Thanh Thao made his mark in poetry as "a dog marks its place by pissing" ("March 12"): that is, boldly, directly, and yet casually, while working in a variety of forms and tones. Today his work is darker, more colloquial, and more ambitious. His passionate poems have strongly influenced the younger generation.

Hoàng Hung's work came to wider public attention in 1988 when the Renovation Movement published his first poetry collection, *The Sea Horse*, with the publisher *Tre*, which means "youth." This controversial collection provoked government mass media with its darkness, solitary characters, and sexual references. The lines, "My friend, where are you going to make love tonight?" and, "A silent wall / A slit / Hair" were considered outrageous. Paying no heed to the controversy, Hoàng Hung published a second collection, *The Man in Search of His Face* (Culture and Information Publisher, 1994), a book which I edited, introduced, and, to some degree, inspired. Indeed, since the Nhan Van controversy, Hoàng Hung has been perhaps the most transgressive figure in contemporary Vietnamese poetry. Although his poetry is based on classical forms, it dares to blend tradition and existentialism yet remains as beautiful as a favorite sonata, hummed under the breath to quell pain or fear. Hoàng Hung is also the best translator of poetry from French and English into Vietnamese; we worked together as the first Vietnamese to translate the poems of Allen Ginsberg in a positive light. Though in comparison to Hung's my own work is rough in texture and tone and looks inward rather than to the social environment, we have both met with fierce disapproval from the official media for our "dark souls" and "nasty language." In my own work, I aim to reflect the emotions of contemporary city life, in which tradition is vanishing or already lost; its path is narrow and indirect, and at times so confining it's hard to take a breath. Influenced strongly by Western culture and my early friendship with Thanh Thao, as well as later friendships with Hoàng Hung and others, my work has its source in the darkness of existentialism and nihilism. A feeling of loneliness permeates my three collections, *The Fish Wharf and The Autumn Evening* (a collaboration with Thanh Thao), *The Empty Space* (Writers Association Publisher, 1992), and the unpublished manuscript *The Somberness*. After reading *The Empty Space*, Duong Thu, the most popular contemporary Vietnamese composer, wrote in *Literature and the Public Review* (July 1992), "This poetry is the saddest that I have read in my life so far." Seized by painful isolation, the persona of my poems is "unable to die, so he has to live," as Hoàng Hung writes in "America." My most significant poetry was written after 1992, while living in Ho Chi Minh City and, later, in very painful circumstances while studying English in the United States.

If Hoàng Hung's poetry is downbeat and melancholy (it is less melancholy, in fact, than that of Hoàng Cam, the poet he most admires) and adopts classical forms, Thanh Thao's poetry creates an intense world of sensation. Because he writes in a modern rather than classical form, his poetry is flexible yet vulnerable, addressing issues as serious as those in Hoàng Hung's work.

The poetry of Dang Dinh Hung, on the other hand, shows little concern for weighty issues and themes. The persona of his work, an intellectual innocent engaged in solitary play and ignorant of the larger world, remains absorbed in ordinary things—bits of trash, the space beneath a table—that others pass every day without paying any attention. Such things are his world and the source of his happiness. Yet while Dang Dinh Hung's poetry expresses no frustration or concern, it possesses a clear, implicit message. Thus far in its history, Vietnam has no poet to compare with this blend of complexity and simplicity. Sometimes Hung's work seems characteristic of the traditional North of Vietnam; however, the modern flexibility of style and presentation in his long poem "The New Horizon" may suggest the work of Franz Kafka or Jean Paul Sartre's later work, such as *Nausea*. Despite his brilliance, not everyone in Vietnamese literary circles thinks of Dang Dinh Hung as a poet. Though he has written some musical works and is officially considered a composer, his central life is in poetry. His poems were not published until one year after his death when his brother, Dang Dinh Ang, a mathematician, and his son, Dang Thai Son, a prominent pianist, arranged for the publication of two of his long poems as separate collections. This was done with the editorial assistance, at different times, of Hoàng Hung and Nguyen Do.

Like Dang Dinh Hung, Van Cao is one of the leaders of the Nhan Van spirit and is therefore responsible for helping to modernize poetry. He abandoned his early lyric style for a more modern style of expression, though his work was not published until very late in the Renovation Movement period. His poetry is notable for its firm and economical use of words. He writes in "The Door"

(1960): "The sound of a knob being turned / Come in / The door opens wide / visible only / the stairs of the family above / and unmoving light a drop of sweat / rolls on my brow." As in most Nhan Van works of that time, Van Cao's poems did not shrink from even the harsher side of reality, such as unsafe living conditions. In just a few words, the poem made people sweat in fear: what is quietly spoken can be the most alarming!

For the most part, the "outsider" poets include those who have never been members of the Writers Association and the members of the Nhan Van group. An exception is Thanh Thao. Though a member of the poetry committee of the Writers Association and head of its provincial branch, he is not a Communist Party member—the only such exception in Vietnam. He has been an "outsider" since the appearance of his first long poem, "A Soldier Speaks of His Generation," the most controversial poem of the Vietnam-American War period.

If a poll were taken to name Vietnam's finest woman poet, readers would likely divide into three camps. Those over forty might choose Xuan Quynh, whose work reflects that generation's experience: the soft, gentle voices of lovers, the sky always as blue as their eyes—but always in the context of the bombing, starvation, and disease associated with the American War. Readers between thirty and forty years of age who love Western culture, modern literature, and are somewhat intellectual may prefer the work of Nhat Le. Ironically, Nhat Le has never looked at herself as a poet, never been popular, and, although several of her poems have appeared in some reviews and newspapers, never published a poetry collection. Regardless, her poems remain the most modern of her generation, and she is seen as a leader among contemporary women poets. But her self-isolation, both her choice and her fate, makes it difficult to answer her own question, "what's strong enough to hang upside down by" ("When I'm Twenty-Three"). Still, her poems work toward such questions. Nhat Le is truly unique in the history of Vietnamese poetry with her poems that are both sensitive in feeling and imaginatively daring.

Readers closer to twenty, with their fast-paced, sometimes risky lifestyle, may identify most with Vi Thuy Linh, the twenty-five-year-old who is among the most popular poets now writing in Vietnam. Vi Thuy Linh's work is fearless; contained only by its lyricism, her poetry focuses on sex as a means of expressing not only her own life but also the lifestyle of her generation. The emotion of her work emerges primarily from the act of making love, sometimes very directly and brutally. Like a shriek, Vi Thuy Linh's poetry demands attention. Given the treatment of Hoàng Hung and others for their use of sexual references, it's ironic that the public, especially the young, now eagerly enjoys her work without fear of censure.

The Poetry of Southern Vietnam, 1954 to 1975

After being divided into two parts in 1954 and sinking into the bloody American war, the Vietnamese people either retained the poetry of the South (if they were born there) or brought from the North the common poetry inheritance of folk tradition and the values of the New Poetry movement. Because of the continuing New Poetry influence in wartime, most poets sang the same melodies as in the past. One exception was the poet Thanh Tam Tuyen and his group Sang Tao ("Creative"), a collection of poets, writers, and artists of the 1960s. Later influenced by existentialism, Thanh Tam Tuyen wrote the richest and most modern poetry of the group. His poems were memorized by readers in both parts of the country—for example, the line "Outside is crystal sunlight / I call my name to miss myself less." Unfortunately, his work is not available to present in this anthology. We hope that his significant body of work can be made public, through translation, in the future.

Poetry without Borders

Poetry is poetry. If your poetry has quality, who cares if you are capitalist or communist? For a sixty-year period (1945–2005), seventeen poets may not seem much of a "Kingdom of Poetry," as some

Vietnamese poets would call it. Nevertheless, it is a reasonable view of the range of contemporary Vietnamese poetry. This anthology is a chronological retrospective of the best poems of the contemporary period, from those who have carried on the New Poetry, or traditional, style, to those who, in spite of their "outsider" status, have shaped the current wave in Vietnamese writing.

After so many years of English-speaking readers lacking access to the range of expression in Vietnamese poetry, I'm glad to bring its history to light. Now that the task is complete, I can smile happily and think of the Thanh Thao line that I love: "I'm silent as a coconut palm / that doesn't know why it bore fruit!"

BLACK DOG, BLACK NIGHT

Huu Loan (1916–)

Born in Thanh Hoa Province, where he eventually returned to make his living as a farmer and laborer, Huu Loan was an original member of the Nhan Van group but broke with it in 1957. Though he has not written much poetry and has published no collection, Huu Loan's life and work are well known; for half a century, his "The Purple Color of Sim Flowers" has been considered one of the outstanding antiwar poems in contemporary Vietnamese poetry. Like other poets of his time—including Tran Mai Ninh, Tran Dan, Hoàng Cam, and Quang Dung—Huu Loan was influenced by the Russian poet Vladimir Mayakovsky in the strength, directness, and vulnerability of his expression. His poetry also reflects the folklore traditions of central Vietnam and the romantic aspects of modernism. Huu Loan was for a time excluded from the Vietnamese Writers Association, to which he had once belonged, because of his involvement in Nhan Van's call for freedom of speech and press in the late 1950s. In 1988, however, due to *glasnost* in the former Soviet Union, he was restored to membership. In 2005 "The Purple Color of Sim Flowers" won a copyright competition, with the director of an electronics company purchasing the poem for one hundred million Vietnamese dollars (about $6,500). The copyright owner has granted permission to translate and reprint the poem.

THE PURPLE COLOR OF SIM FLOWERS

She had three older brothers in the army,
but some of the younger ones
were still too young to speak
and her hair was still green.

I was in the National Guard,
far from my family,
and loved her as one loves a sister.
On the day of our engagement,
she didn't ask for a new shirt.

I was wearing my army uniform,
boots still muddy from marching.
She smiled prettily
next to her dear husband.
I had traveled from camp
for the wedding but had to leave soon.
Back at the distant camp
I was full of sorrow
about marriage in wartime.
Very few husbands were returning home.
It was the same for me.
How painful love is
for a young woman
who must wait at home so long
sunset after sunset. . . .

But there is no death for
the man in the smoke and fire of battle.
Death comes instead
to the young woman

at the home front.
Returning home,
I didn't see her,
but my mother sat beside her grave in complete darkness.
The wedding flower vase
became a funeral incense vase
covered with the cold.

Her hair was still green
and too short to twist into a bun.
Oh, my love, the last moment of our lives together
we had no chance to listen,
to look at each other,
a single light shining.

Yesterday, you loved purple *sim,*
and your shirt was that color.
Yesterday,
alone
in midnight lamplight,
a small shadow
sewed her husband's shirt.
Yesterday . . .

On a rainy forest evening
three brothers in the northeast battle
heard news of their sister's death
before news of her wedding.
The autumn wind blew, making waves on the dark green river.
Someday her little sister will grow up
and stare at her picture in surprise
as early autumn wind blows the yellow grass around her tombstone.

Marching in the evening,
crossing the *sim* hills,
which are long and endless,
the purple color of *sim*
makes the evening purple and empty.
I look at myself, shirt bursting at the shoulder,
and sing
in the color of *sim,*
"My shirt broke its threads at the seam.
My wife died young,
but my mother is very old
so she can't . . ."

Te Hanh (1920–)

A native of Quang Ngai and a member of the Vietnamese Writers Association, Te Hanh is retired and lives in Hanoi. Among his many awards is the distinguished Ho Chi Minh Prize he received in 1996. Te Hanh was the youngest poet of the New Poetry movement (1933–1945) and continued writing into the 1980s, publishing thirteen collections of poems rich in feeling and varied in mood. His approach to his subjects, even political matters, is gentle, pure, warm, natural, and harmonious, as well as ultimately grounded in the senses. Perhaps that groundedness explains why he "lives" longer than others, in poetry and in life.

HANOI WITHOUT YOU

Now Hanoi is without you
I walk along the streets looking for the past

This street next to a park
makes me remember waiting for you as if for the wind—we were
    familiar but not close

This street, on that moonlit evening
when you and I walked for a while talking in silence

This street where I came to look for you
makes people think I'm looking for a shade tree

I follow the streets here and there
And love Hanoi, even though it's empty without you

THE OLD GARDEN

The old garden, in which the trees grow greener day by day
The old mother's hair grayer moment by moment
Now you and I are on opposite sides of a cause
Do you ever return to that old garden?

Both of us like sunny days and rainy days
which differ in their length like the moon and sun
like evening and morning star
Do you ever return to that old garden?
Both of us like the summer lotus and autumn carnation
We like persimmon in October and *longan* in May
You follow the birds returning in August
I follow them when March is over

Returning home on a spring day
You heard Mom say that I once picked guavas at home
You looked up at that shade tree; wind whistled
in the leaves the way voices faintly call me home
Returning again on a summer day
I hear Mom say that you once washed clothes at the well
I look down into its smooth depths
Like a mirror, the water reflects my lonely shadow

In the old garden the trees seem greener day by day
The old mother's hair grayer moment by moment
You and I are on opposite sides of a cause
Do you ever return to that old garden?

MISSING MY HOME RIVER

My home country has a dark green river
Its water is like a mirror in which bamboo can see its hair
My soul is a summer noon
covered in shadow all the way to the shining river

How many days, months, and souvenirs
has that water held in its streaming?
Oh river, which cleanses my life,
I'll keep you forever like a new lover
You belong to my country home, my youth,
and to the beautiful South of Vietnam
When the edge of the bamboo forest was filled with chattering
     birds
when the water surface was flecked by jumping fish
our group of five or seven friends
flocked like young birds to swim in the river
I opened my hands to embrace the water to my chest
The river opened to embrace me to its belly
Then we grew up; everyone is different in his way of life
Some net fish on the river from morning to night
Some hoe and plow under rain and sun on their fields
I left my family to carry a gun and fight the enemy
But today, as suddenly as rain goes back its source, the wind to
     its ocean,
I return to the river with fondness in my heart

Oh my home country, I have been living in the heart of the North
Touching my heart, I can hear it speak
two soulful sounds, two words: "The South."
I miss so much the yellow of that sunlight
How can I forget the dark blue of that sky?

I miss even the people back home whom I haven't met
Some day at noon I'll stand at a line of trees
suddenly welling up with emotion
as the cool presence of my home river
makes my soul flow like a creek running in
Oh, my home country, my soul is like the river,
South or North, both streaming in one direction—
impossible to block!
I will be back where I want to be
I will return to my home river
I will return to my river's love

Van Cao (1923–1992)

Van Cao was born in the city of Hai Phong and raised in Hanoi. An accomplished poet, Cao was also an artist and one of the most prominent composers in Vietnamese history; he wrote the country's national anthem, as well as many well-known romantic songs. In 1996, he won the Ho Chi Minh Prize, the highest award given for the arts in Vietnam. Van Cao was a member of the Nhan Van with Dang Dinh Hung and others; however, because of the anthem's popularity and his social and political adeptness, he was less restricted than other members. Though he began writing poetry in 1942, Van Cao did not publish a collection until 1988, when *glastnost* liberalization enabled him to release *The Grass*. After his death, a second collection, *Van Cao's Poetry*, was published. With the exception of "Hai Phong," his poems are short but also very thoughtful and emotional in tone. They explore the tension of those who, though they have experienced great pain in life, remain silent, unable to tell anyone.

YOUR FACE

In the long days
that remain, only your face
is bright, pure, and calm
even though you and I
have never been satisfied
But throughout it all
your face
is a crescent moon at night, a forest catching fire

Farther along our way
I lie you down in a meadow
and see the endless beauty of wild green grass

Farther along our way
I lie you down on the slopes of mountains
to see again their soft curves

Farther along the way
your face is a well
and in its depths I find pearls
How bright your face, so pure and calm
from our first moment to our last

SOMETIMES

Sometimes
I'm alone with a knife in the forest's dark night,
but unafraid of tigers.

Sometimes,
hearing leaves fall in daylight,
I wonder why I am startled.

And sometimes
the tears can't even run out of my eyes.

EMPTY

the cries of roosters rise
causing the last stars to fall
a sound in my soul
contains pain and happiness
like a flaming piece of steel
plunged in a pot of cold water

the sounds of singing chase each other on mountaintops
a lonely lake
stops the volcano's mouth

A BEER JOINT

Many people come here
They find their crowd
a small vault of sky under red and green umbrellas

drinking to be as empty as a cup
drinking to end a day which is ending
drinking to end a year which is almost over
still licking their lips

They thirst for beer or lives
or the crowds
walking outside
Inside these crowds is one solid
crowd after another. . . .

Under the red and green umbrellas
the cups of beer bubble up
People lick their lips

THE DOOR

The sound of a knob being turned
Come in

The door opens wide

Visible only
the stairs of the family above
and unmoving light

A drop of sweat
rolls on my brow

NIGHTLY RESTAURANT

For Nguyen Sang

It's not for a glass of *Ruou* and the cold food of a bad restaurant
I come back every night.
I come back
because I want to see the still, yellow light in the darkness of that
slum
beside the railroad tracks covered with coal dust,
destitute faces that come night after night to drink *Ruou,* talking
louder than in the daytime when they have to make a living;
because I want to see the shape of the elderly owner's stooped back
and his flock of children, who are growing
as fast as the last five years have blown by;
because as a friend I'm familiar with all of his celebrations and
am dear to his family; because I miss a nasty *Ruou* table with
worm-eaten chairs and bamboo walls tacked with colorful
pictures
cut from old newspapers that divide the family from
their neighbors, a couple given to cursing and
violence;
because I miss my seat, the mood, and my slightly drunken
tottering night walks along the railroad tracks.

But no, no, it's not that; I've never seen the light of the nightly
restaurant, in which the faces resemble the earth, reflected
through flame as white as the silk thread of the elderly owner's
hair; not his noisy and rude children;
not because I miss my seat in the dilapidated house where it rains
on the *Ruou* table.

I come back
because I see myself here, only me
at midnight returning alone,
crossing the railroad tracks dusty with coal;
because what I've found I have never seen!

THREE VARIATIONS AT SIXTY-FIVE YEARS OLD

On sad days I'm unable to speak
I can only just find my existence

I

A man gives me a knife
Looking through the window into the night
a black empty space
I don't know what it's used for

I throw the knife
into that space
Perhaps I mean only mischief

Suddenly the sound of collapsing
Someone is struck in the heart and dies

I don't know that man
I don't want to be a killer

I only know the darkness
that I throw

II

I walk on a street
Suddenly people stare at me
Someone yells, "A thief!"
I run
I escape

Why do I run?
        I don't understand myself
The entire street runs after me
        Cars run after me
I run for my life
almost reaching my fate
before slumping down
Waking sweaty
I recognize myself—not guilty

III

I fall into a spiderweb
It wraps me tightly
no way of getting out
I'm like a silkworm
in this life

I want to break the net
but my arms are far too few!

FIVE UNREAL MORNINGS

Each night the rooftops give birth to wings
and dreams under an immense, starry sky

I

When I wake in the morning
the entire street has gone away
no walking shadows
just the deep, intense silence of a lake
Like the mouth of a volcano
the land's surface is the color of fire and brick
I'm leaving to look for you
searching traces of the paths
where often we have gone
Endlessly I call you and call you
Our century stopped right here
but where are you?
That other century still exists
but on this earth
here in the everyday
I call you and call you

II

This morning no bird sings
It seems unreal
I walk soundlessly
The city and I are silent
People
can be recognized by their dark eyes only
Cars run mutely
Why? Why?

Nobody looks at my mouth; I scream silently
In shock, I run along the ground
lonely
in a city of speechless people
Why? Why? No talking
no sound, no life
Why is this city like a desert
without a whisper of wind?
People seem frozen in place
but pass quickly
Perhaps here
they are exiled in silence

III

This is not me waking this morning
Someone else breathes in me
In front of me
a room, half-night and half-day, emerges into
a city half-moon and half-sun
so that I am two people who think about each other
are each other's enemy
two extremes of the spirit
who endure each other
try to harm each other
who don't know day or night, truth or lie,
the me who is not me

IV

This morning the city is a lie, a festival
People wearing masks wander around
dancing step by step
Happiness appears in young leaves

In spring
shade trees are pearl green on streets
Ruou, silk, wool, and stiff paper flowers
twinkle on the sidewalks
The masks say hello to each other
In spring, children
rosy as dolls;
flatten bottle caps into coins, play spring games
with wide, round, amazing eyes—
so happy
But look!
Why do sweat and tears
appear on each mask?
All the people
weep on their own stiff paper faces

V

Locking every door
in a crystal room
Please come closer to me
your body warm as a stove
to make the spring less cold
Like a young *khuyen* that lies in my hands
shivering
like two young branches
filled with spring sap
and blossoming rosebuds
we go secretly to spring

Hoàng Cam (1922–)

A poet and playwright born in Thuan Thanh, Bac Ninh Province, Hoàng Cam now lives in Hanoi. He has published seven poetry collections as well as several plays and French translations. A former director of the Vietnamese Army Concerts, a music performance series, he was a member of Nhan Van and spent several months as a prisoner in the notorious "Hanoi Hilton." However, in February, 2007, one month before Hoàng Cam sank into a serious illness, the president of Vietnam awarded him the National Prize for his poetry collection *Returning to Kenh Bac* (possession of which had led to Hoàng Hung's imprisonment in 1982). With assistance Hoàng Cam was able to attend the awards ceremony in spite of his illness. Three other Nhan Van members were awarded the same prize at the ceremony.

Hoàng Cam's melancholy poems are reminiscent of Vietnam's romantic period, which was deeply influenced by nineteenth-century French poetry. Among his poems is the very popular "The Other Side of Duong River," which, while informed by the formal style and voice of Mayakovsky (as were many other Vietnamese poets of that time), also adhered to the melodies of Bac Ninh folk songs. Bac Ninh songs are similar to the geisha songs of Japan and, to some extent, the blues songs of African-Americans—sweet, melancholy, and with an extreme hopelessness that suggests late French romanticism. Poems in the Bac Ninh style are among the best the Vietnamese imagination has to offer, both accessible to readers and easy to remember and sing along with.

I LIVE IN QUAN HO CIRCLE

I'm a Quan Ho resident
My mother's home village is on a riverbank
separated from my father's
by a bright stream

The eighteen-year-old girl of Xim village
sang beautifully and famously in her region
When she sang
couples in love would immediately gather and sift rice straws
    to make their bed mats
Women unhappy to be engaged
would return their demand gifts

A young student
walked nervously back and forth
then straight across the river
hoping to see her

The *betel* and *areca* with grilled pink rice hadn't yet matched
when shreds from the wedding firecrackers littered a rainy
    and muddy alley
The matchmaker chewing *betel*
hadn't finished the first bunch
made in the shape of phoenix wings
before the bad news came that the girl hated her husband

and all the gossip that followed

The groom said he would love her even if she quit singing
She looked down and scratched her bra
Leaning on a corner post, she breathlessly listens

to her friends' Quan Ho singing.
The wind carries it into her room,
which is locked against the song.
She prayed and begged in tears
her singing still jailed
Turning her face away from his on the pillow
the wife waited for the Pleiades to show her the way
then left with her lover
who had been sailing as she sang under Quan Ho moonlight

Ten years after that lonely wedding
the husband missed her singing very much
He looked for her after a Quan Ho festival
asking please come back and let him love her

She touched her first gray hair
beneath the rounded rim of her veil

Both suddenly felt that their new loves had run dry
and returned to the ones they had loved first

I was born from that love
When my mother dressed me in a thin diaper
I exhausted both her breast milk
and her singing

I grew up
inheriting my mother's beautiful voice
and her bright eyes
but my heavy bones
drag me along the curve of my fate

The songs my mother sang gave me white wings
that flew a thousand times to rescue my life
sometimes bleeding
but never breaking the chain

Young gums feel pain and can barely bite the chain
but today in a finished poem
a whole jaw emerged

Couples in love and their children
All over my home country
lovers are flying
But hope's horizon is still foggy

From a distant ocean, my mother calls me,
her voice still drowned by the tide

THE DIEU BONG LEAF

Wearing a wavy *Dinh Bang* skirt
she dejectedly walked back and forth to look for it
in a field in the evening
among rice stubble

She said
Whoever finds a *Dieu Bong* Leaf
I will call him my husband

Two days later I found a Leaf
She knitted her brows
It wasn't the one

The following winter I found that Leaf
She shook her head
and looked at the river covered in sunlight

On her wedding day
I found that Leaf
She smiled
The thread is kept warm by the needle's eye
When she had three kids
again I found the Leaf
Her hands covered her face like blindness

Since that time
I have carried that Leaf
from mountains to oceans
My home wind howls
Dieu Bong oh . . . !
Oh *Dieu Bong* . . . !

Tran Dan (1924–2001)

Tran Dan was a poet, translator, and winner of the National Book of the Year Award in poetry. He published six literary works in his lifetime, including poetry collections. A member of the Vietnamese Writers Association, he was a leader of the Nhan Van movement as well as the revolutionary group Da Dai; unfortunately, he spent a long time in jail and "reform camp" for his activities. Once he attempted suicide by cutting his throat in Hanoi's Hoa Lo jail, known to Americans as the "Hanoi Hilton." Like many others in the anticolonial period (1945–1954), he was heavily influenced by the poetry of Mayakovsky, writing strongly voiced poems centered in political concepts. A large number of Tran Dan's unpublished works, including his short poems (now considered among the most important he wrote after 1954 under the influence of existentialism and late romanticism), are very political and therefore susceptible to investigation by authorities. The works of Tran Dan and Dang Dinh Hung were influential to each other, with both also relating to the Nhan Van group as a whole in their desire to seek a connection between the soul and one's style as an artist. Because Tran Dan's strong opinions were expressed in ways accessible to all citizens, his work received a good deal of public attention. In February of 2007, the Nhan Van writers Tran Dan, Hoàng Cam, Le Dat, and Phung Quan were awarded the National Prize for their lifetime contribution to literature, an honor that serves as a kind of exemption granted by the president of Vietnam.

A circle of people always surrounds a naked man.

Creation is total force, action, and suddenness including the
scrotum, which is involved in creation also.

Building a poetry collection is like breaking into a prison.

The *Ruou* is so strong that it hurts the mouth, like the vulva of
a girl who hasn't had sex for a long time—one that explodes
is always the best.

When we touch the air
it is without scar,
but the nipple is a scar of relation between the mother and her
children
and
the human face
is an external scar
for the many palpable scars inside.

Worry
must go to heaven
lonely,
very lonely.

The falling rain
doesn't need a translator.

Everyday I eat a horizon.

I am in pain because
each person is a trial.

THE BLIND PATH

I am still me! Cracks appear on my forehead
and disappear in a lusty night and the smooth sweat of kissing and
    opium lamplight
dry as a yellow curve of evening in which leaves are red as hearts
I lose my temper! As a cloud flies out of Hang Song Street
on which I leave a sad footstep that has not scabbed over yet

Somebody asks me, please, how can I escape from my millions
    of selves?
The tinkling street obsesses me every morning
and a buzz obsesses me in the evening

Every night rain falls into my heart
I hear the ticking of the old clock

A cigarette burns my lips
Except for his eyes, a man is buried in a thumbprint of darkness
A funeral candle drops its pus in the night

On a summer noon, nuns who wear blue shirts
open their skirts to catch lice in a park
When the lights are off, darkness is a kind of convent
Suddenly but meticulously I
stop reading the Bible to pick the scab
of an old sadness that is still unhealed in my heart

How can I explain it?
I haven't fallen in love yet I'm already out of love
the way a river loses itself traveling to the sea

Who? Who can create for me
a world in harmony?
Who can build a bridge to heaven?
Please give me one day—an entire day of childishness!
Please give me any street corner where the haze falls naturally,
    all by itself
But, I can't . . . I can't!
Don't force me to make a living in Europe
Not Asia either
How about Africa?
No, no! I get confused
Why do I divide into five continents?
So I will be able to count all of them
I am like a fool,
counting everything but never above the number one
I am . . . OK stop! I'm not going to play with you guys any longer
I'm leaving! Farewell!
Leave me alone! Leave me alone!

I don't have enough pain to last to the end of a long life
I don't have enough love
to love this unsteady earth

Forgive me! I haven't broken anything yet
only a small piece of life—my own lives
Farewell! Farewell!
I have never owned anything
but if I had anything
please allow me to postpone it until tomorrow
if tomorrow still exists!
        Mother! Oh, please stay home! I'm leaving. . . .

NEW YEAR

Hey, New Year,
how can you be so new?
You can't just pretend to be new by cheering and lecturing,
and don't be new carelessly,
new on some days
then returning to what you are—old,
old and wrinkled,
as you've always been.
You're paler than the useless things
that cats bring back,
that dogs bring forth.

Come on, New Year!
Let's be new honestly, as before.

THE SPEECHLESS LIGHT POLE

We come into life
all at the same level,
with only a flat-rate ticket.
Any kind of favor
reeks of unfairness.

In an unfriendly cosmos,
I have had a satellite
and a blue station,
then a purple one.

The bird trap is so confining
I fly in every direction.
It hurts my head.

I have a talent for being silent,
like a speechless light pole
on a corner of a street—it's so naïve!

A MAN MADE OF FLESH

As is being confirmed,
I'm a pillar of male muscle.
My most intellectual part
lives near
my ass.

In other words, my life
has been influenced by my throat.

I suddenly swell so big, I can stand up vertically in excitement—
like the heat of a cake in the oven or the torridness of a chorus,
I can feel hot or cold, heavy and frozen.

And sometimes
I'm able to walk.

Well, I know how to walk. . . .
No, "walking" isn't quite the word.

I move carefully beneath khaki pockets and sausage muscle
in fresh darkness. Only a tiny eye and nose of flesh remain
uncovered.

I'm in a rush.
The girls' chubby cheeks twist as they walk. Flesh
girls. Undressed, a look can pass through them; all
are virgin, *angélique.*

Honestly, sometimes I just stare at them, squint my eyes, and feel
shy to imagine it.

My goodness! God is so wise, he was on fire when he designed and created me. Eve touches me all day.

It's even scarier if I'm not given underwear.

So this is me.

To be cool all summer. Here are the flesh faucet, flesh shower and the bathtub of silken, sniffed, and tightened flesh. A flesh crab crawls on the floor with slow flesh claws. Its flesh pillar stands suddenly, nakedly, with a string of eggs. Completely deadpan nude of a pound of flesh.

The clock rings the flesh time.

A flesh couple wrestle each other on a bench; they're stretching, scratching, slapping and breaking into loving flesh. Molesting and biting as the rain storms down, they are torn apart, as if struck by a stout wave.

As a piano's quiet keys suddenly begin screaming, they suck and throw each other, as if throwing cold sand. They sing and cry and pass out in an orchestra's soaking chorus.

Turning
the opposite
of flesh.

The *table de nuit* hugs itself; the flesh room opens its window to see the flesh stars. They flesh themselves obsessively to break their bells and widen everything hugely. Over there, the spring drizzle breathes flesh humus.

Here's a flesh rest area for drinking beer in a flesh life. Here is a flesh refill overflowing onto the ground, on which I write then throw away messy. The pen drinks and vomits manly flesh ink.

> **A** girl with a bamboo basket is a tight flesh bell
> running in circles.
> The rain falls around her hips and receding chin.
> **A** fleshy man jogging, whose flesh falls down to his
> heels like seeds of grain husking themselves,
> becoming a flour that blends with water.

I often look at flesh myself, for example in the morning, between the sun smiling and spreading the hips and legs of young girl rice.

The moist-flesh model lies down on a hammock, her lips kissing its edge, as it swings wet onto the easel, making the flesh artist turn the color of hot water.

I walk down to the flesh pond to wash my flesh face from morning to evening. The sunrise exhales a moist flesh air.

> **I**'d love to have flesh
> a different one
> taking off her underwear
> shyly
> shyly
> an open circle.
> Messy, messy. The naked poet puts flesh into flesh
> mud, so pure it's transparent as crystal; flesh vision
> stares into flesh underwear.

> **Oh**, no! I'm gonna die . . . *Parc de lune!*

The hairy-fleshed man carefully opens a flesh slit, from which a sputnik gradually swells among massive, disorderly, breathing stars.

I'm heavy, heavy as sound, heavy from my flesh face to flesh feet; I have been dragging many sidewalks and many kilometers. They're all dirty.

> Oh, it's silent from the beginning to the end of the street,
> on which, in slight rain, there's a light pole of flesh.
> Faintly,
> Faintly,
> the flesh-light.

> I'm solid,
> so-
> lid.

> I'm going by f-le-sh . . .
> for many rainy kilos
> with dimming flesh eyes.

Dang Dinh Hung (1924–1990)

Born in Ha Dong, Hanoi, Dang Dinh Hung was a composer and artist who was also recognized as a modern poet and the father of the prominent and successful pianist Dang Thai Son, the first Asian to win the Chopin competition (1980). (The International Chopin Piano Competition is held once a year. The award is one of the highest honors given to pianists.) Dang Dinh Hung was a former political commissar of the Army Concert series, at which time he was involved in the Nhan Van group of writers, composers, artists and playwrights who sought freedom of speech and the press during the Vietnamese Cultural Revolution of the 1950s. They published a review, *Giai Pham,* or "Fine Works." As a result, most of them were eliminated from their local writers associations, and, to be "reformed," sent to live and work apart from their families. Laboring under harsh conditions on farms or in factories, they were treated like prisoners. Freed during a period of "good reform," Dang Dinh Hung found himself with no partner (his wife, a music professor and pianist, had divorced him), no job, and no publishing opportunities. He lived in poverty, nearly starving, until 1988, the year of *glasnost,* by which time his son was a well-known pianist. Dang Dinh Hung wrote some of his poetry in the hospital after serving the rest of his sentence on parole, or "prison without walls." His work has strongly influenced the "outside" poets of Vietnam, but mainstream practice tends to run in the same direction for a long time—as long as a century—before its next turning point; therefore, Vietnamese poetry may have yet to feel the full influence of Dang Dinh Hung's emotionally expressive style. His poetry is the most complicated in Vietnam's history, and its complexity is heightened by his incorporation of surrealist images, Western existentialism, and a tone of solitude that he called "the perfect loneliness." At times Dang Dinh Hung's speakers seem almost insane. His melancholy has also drawn comparisons to the traditional Quan Ho folk songs.

While Dang Dinh Hung has achieved fame, his poetry is sometimes considered "lookable" rather than "touchable," and few poets and readers feel confident in approaching and analyzing his work. It's humorous that, while most people are uncomfortable in talking about his poems, they are also reluctant to acknowledge their lack of understanding. In this respect, his work is reminiscent of that of postmodern American poet John Ashbery. To the Western reader, Dang Dinh Hung's work may seem prophetic of postmodernism, as seen in the lines below: "Its distance has no measure. That's its only feature." Dang Dinh Hung did not write many poems, but just after his death, in 1991, two of his book-length poems, *The New Horizon* and *O Mai,* were published. After they appeared, the division among critics was sharp—they were seen either as perfect poems or not poems at all.

FROM *THE NEW HORIZON* (1)

I'm leaving again . . .
    on the tray of my back's shadow, a blackboard in front of my
eyes and a chalk circle
beneath my feet, which is sticky like the number 8 lying down, like
    a smooth magnet,
like a rice grain that will grow into who knows what.

    I will know the endlessness of Epicure's crotch, fat and naked,
while around him,
loudly dancing, are blue and yellow poker cards on which praying
mantises land then jump randomly! They
joyfully ride on the backs of cards as stiff as the Karma would have
them!

    I don't know,
maybe I should include the dry cracks in jackfruit
I was looking for behind a mirror, nothing there
but pain from all the small, trivial acts of my life,
slurping bowl after bowl of insipidness and softness
but so happily. . . .

    I carry
very gently
a sloping tray of rain on my back.
A friend named Alpha carries me, one two three . . . I carry Alpha
back, thin and almost weightless. Because there is a drumming in my
    chest, a beating.

    While spending an hour looking into the lens of a hand-
cranked movie camera,

I see the world's horizontal and vertical axes are only foolish
    distances.
An ink pot floats over the Capital Letters, which of course dissolve
in ink, but I still
haven't written my note.
I forgot
completely forgetting logarithms, broken curves, four table legs,
beneath which I clamped my teeth
to a corner, crunching on cubical sunsets like wounds of air or
balloons randomly flying.

FROM *THE NEW HORIZON* (II)

Again I don't know why that Alpha bird perches on the gable of
Meta's house. And it hangs around. It's like when I was a little
boy. I stood on a chair on tiptoe but still not high enough to
look into a wooden crate, in craven hunger, at Alpha's favorite
food, covered by a bamboo mesh, round as the season itself.

From the acute angle *A*, I go the frightening abyss of *V*. Every time
I arrive, memory returns me to the very beginning. Someone
says: at the horizon, at the point *YZ*, there is no measure or
distance but I know what it is—a folding Chinese lantern, my
own personal favorite. Its distance has no measure. That's its
only feature.

I arrive at the New Horizon, an evening with no Alpha,
where I stand
on the plateau of Meta

                            arriving angrily in the morning at a horizon
where an empty train station informs me of messages from
Alpha it's Teta that tells me like a midwife a tiny fish swimming
in a stranger ocean my pencil moves back and forth and into
my room with no knocking door what an impolite pencil
writing words like a baby works a breast always raising its head
to look at a book a large pregnant belly appears with her face
and washing basin on that horizon also

Yes, I'm tired of the New Horizon.
Having no influence over the calendar,
I got very old.

I arrive at the New Horizon biting a fig, strange in its blue unripeness, but the lightbulb of my first encounter with the curious distances of Alpha-Omega is as ripe as can be.
And how strange it tastes! Waiting for the crunching footsteps of Teta, I realize that Alpha, like a shoulder, is also a number, one half incomplete because it opens so quickly, the other one closed, so that I must chase and fasten them together, as one would join two seasons.

                                        I'm
alive,
my every finger pushing a key with its sound of bells into a lock in the golden memory of air; to my surprise, every time I see my face in a mirror, an aria resounds.

FROM *THE NEW HORIZON* (III)

The New Horizon is right here beneath my bed a heavy rain is
right here beneath a table and in a wooden crate the navy uses
for shipping and in many symbols of the Red Sea sails spread out
like bras and in the ardent perfume of last year's wedding now it is
dried under the sun and put out for show the sail-bras are sailing
but the light poles are not.

    The light poles are dancing *plinc! plonc!* with their karma, and
stopping to take a shower of happy water, then looking down on me.

                                             These

lumière poles
seem slow and heavy
because traveling to the New Horizon nobody can hold a trail of
cigarette smoke, which turns round and round a circle, how can
I draw that blue!
The New Horizon puts its legs on prisms of a grandfather clock
that puts on airs to move its firm and strong muscle together
with its empty bottom to show its shy thighs and its intellect
as drowsy flowers at noon on the new horizon.
Together, one by one, lip by lip
a cloth and a tailor's wooden ruler
a male bat and a banana-leaf pip
are beautiful, eyeing eyes and penciling spiral lines
on sketch paper. . . .
Carrying on my shoulder magnificent decorative bulbs then
throwing them, I'm running to a party.
My original hair looks askance at me, who's now sweaty and nasty.
The hair bites half . . . bites three-fourths, bites a little more . . .
only a tiny bit remains. Come on! Just the last bit. Free. *Gratis-
dernière catouse!* Suck!

       I'm leaving, looking for a cork to be my friend.
But wait a second! Let's talk to it first.

In fact, my desire is large, like a piece of chalk that wants to take a warm shower, rub my feet and dry my body with a new towel.
Actually,
I'm already 80 years old.
How many times I've lost my teeth then cut new ones, and cut my hair too.
Once,
I recognized the bottom of a bottle I lost at a recycling center when I heard faint sounds of boxes and metals
and the truth of the matter is
when looking at clogs, I mostly care about the tightness of the straps.
If I were 40 years old, I'd have 40 shoulders.
42
is having a long back
40 is 40 food trays
40 chopsticks
every time I need to eat
every time I clean my mouth
40 bars of soap

But
I'm just 50
I'm young again
probably I dyed my hair
50 already
Do I need 50 bags of candy?

If it's raining, a big bag.
I'm all stressed out, want to snatch some scars
I'm 50
50 OK?
50 losses
50 profits

50 razors
So, I still need
exactly 50 lips

It's quite true, 50 is a century broken in half
·Hey, century, come here, I'll show you around!

Carry me quickly to 91
almost back to the starting line
91 lost chances
completely lost
·Everybody has to smile
Even a bottle smiles
91 times a baby learns how to roll over
and smile
91 times to stop sucking
91 times a baby, I scurry around in a flea market filled with mallow
91 times I'm caught
91 times I'm jostled by the crowd, my teeth completely lost, I pick
them up in my own light
So, at Highway 91, at the crossing
1 year old
I cry
91 smoking
pensively . . .
91 times forgiven!

Good-bye! I'm leaving! I'm arriving at the New Horizon like Alpha
one brown evening, do you remember?
In the Teta Restaurant I eat new silent symbols, feeding myself one
at a time with the fork of memory,
in which I am barefoot walking step by step! From the heights of
91, I look down and eat, smelling the strange shoulder of 1.

Have you ever failed to keep a meeting 91 times?
91 times been frightened
by the littlest things
like taking a shower?
91 years old, I whisper to my ear, begging:
Please let me go to the New Horizon . . .
Because friendliness is a small horizon
where three roads meet at 91 and 1.
I smile:
91 bets
and I haven't won once!

Good-bye, I'm leaving! I return to being a 1 year old:
white beans, black beans drop around a wooden pillow,
from the head of the bed down to the floor, and they sprout, not
caring if a little kid wets the bed; a painful night doesn't leave
overnight, you have to dry a bed to use it.
1 year old, I'm on Teta Street watching two little Alpha-Tetas press
their lips together at the beginning of a trail where a noodle
restaurant is crowded on Sunday with fathers and their kids.

1 year old, I walk with a member of my family through a park to
the hospital, where I see a New Horizon of friendships, friends to
friends, wives to husbands, and difficulty to courage; all of them
are simple compared to the normal life of a spout's pouty mouth,
and several funny faces in a barber shop in line to be gelled, to
have their scars of time removed, scars like potatoes rolling up and
down the road to look for their New Horizon, which is right in
their room with lovely beds with smooth stairs and lights which
usually forget to say hello and good-bye. . . .

Yesterday, I visited Alpha.
He wasn't home.

Oh, I've been friendly for a long time, how come we still want
a handful of midnight stars to sprinkle on the New Horizon?

What is a life?
Why do I carry my luggage and continuously travel and travel to
the New Horizon?

Xuan Quynh (1942–1988)

A member of the Vietnamese Writers Association and editor for literary reviews, Xuan Quynh won the National Book of the Year Award in 1990 for her poetry collection *Co May Flower* and the National Prize for Lifetime Contribution in Literature in 2001. Xuan Quynh, born in Ha Bac Province, is by far the most popular twentieth-century female Vietnamese poet. Her life ended mysteriously in a tragic accident which also killed her husband, Luu Quang Vu, a poet and famous playwright, and their son. Xuan Quynh's poems embody the values of the New Poetry movement: simple and romantic yet complicated by her own life experiences at a turning point of Vietnamese history. Xuan Quynh published at least ten poetry collections. Her work is like a hornet sting to the heart.

LOVE POEM IN LATE AUTUMN

On the horizon a mass of white clouds flies
but yellow leaves remain a little longer
When will they leave their forest
as autumn follows behind them?
In an immense river of leaves
autumn flows to the ocean
Now it is gone with its daisies
but only you and I

only you and I
belong to autumn's past
A breath of *Heo May* wind blows us back
changing everything
A familiar path becomes strange
Leaves of grass look up at the clouds
We're going home with our foggy faces

The coldness passes through our hands
But our loving is like a corridor of trees
bent by many rainstorms
Our loving is a river
after the flood has passed

Time is the wind
of a season; days and months hurry
The years hurry also
but only in you and me

Only in you and me
loving remains unchanged
Look, over there
Other new couples
feel the *Heo May* wind passing

SONG OF MYSELF

I'm not a fool to wish it were golden—
my heart, which has been so wise,
you're the kind that doesn't care about fortune
If needed, you'd throw it all away

And I don't wish it to be like the sun
When the sunset comes it will be dead
So you walk alone in the long, silent night
your heart far away from my heart

I return to my original heart
which knows how to recover shed blood
knows to recover all things that are lost
and diminish love's separation

I return to my original heart
which knows to thirst for your desires
knows to feel through knowledge
how to love you and how you love me

There are many storms this autumn
but people don't close their train windows
The wild field and forest are so dark
I seem to be lost in the forest of you

I worry about what will happen
The heart beats of things that are speechless
The heartbeat seems to be starving—
a glimmering, lonesome flame

I return to my original heart
The beating of its blood is like anyone else's
It will stop, of course, when I die
but will love you even when I'm gone

A LULLABY

A flower vase sleeps on a desk
Look, a book is closed and the lamplight is tired
Let them sleep, my lover
A strange ship lands in a port
The night sky leans over the rooftops,
and the blue sea dreams of land

If you are dreaming, do you see me?
A small carnation is at home in the earth
Bamboo sheaths drop onto their hedge
After visiting its sea, a river returns to its forest home
and a road runs where there is no road

Let the lovely forehead sleep
A painting sleeps and a wall is silent
Let the rock sleep softly
because the feet are hard
Time and the wind blow gently
Love is a meadow of flowers under the sky
My hand is held in yours
If a hundred creeks and a thousand passes are blocked we will still
   pass through

Hoàng Hung (1942–)

A poet and translator, Hoàng Hung was born in Bac Ninh Province, earned a degree in literature at Hanoi Pedagogic University, and now lives in Ho Chi Minh City and Hanoi. His father was the first medical doctor to practice in Indochina. Hoàng Hung is among the most well-known literary figures who is not a member of the Vietnamese Writers Association. In 1998 he received the National Book of the Year Award in the field of translation, and in 2007 his latest poetry collection, *Hanh Trinh (The Journey)*, was named Book of the Year by the Hanoi Writers Association.

Beginning in 1982, Hoàng Hung spent thirty-nine months in jail and "reform camp" because he owned and was suspected of wanting to give a prohibited Hoàng Cam poetry manuscript to a friend working in the French Embassy. After his release from jail, Hoàng Hung had to support himself and his family by selling cameras. He has since worked for many newspapers as an editor, staff writer, and translator (from French and English). In two poetry collections, *Ocean Horse* and *A Man in Search of His Face,* Hoàng Hung was seen as "beating up" his Vietnamese readers, most of them traditional in approach, by mixing sex, nihilism, and a love of surrealism with classic poetic forms. Hoàng Hung's poetry has been influenced by Lorca, Apollinaire, and Pasternak, and inspired by Hoàng Cam, though Hoàng Hung's poems are darker and more powerful than Hoàng Cam's. Hoàng Hung's poetry strikes a lighter note at times in its melodic use of Quan Ho folk songs. His work has encouraged young, educated poets to take risks—especially after the appearance of *A Man in Search of His Face,* when many young poets imitated the Hoàng Hung style.

UNTITLED POEM [RAIN MAKES DREAMS]

For Hoàng Cam

Rain makes dreams
A barrel full of the bad old days
I'm leaving
Wind, oh the wind!

A silent wall
A slit
Hair

WAKING IN HON GAI

I wake suddenly at night; what time is it?
It's so sultry. Waves have no measure,
and the mountain leans too close to my head.
Clouds, like faces, are pale and exhausted.
Frightened and nervous, I leap to my feet.
Hurry, dawn, bring the shining morning
before the rock comes down!

THE MADWOMAN

Carrying a broken brick on her head
she walks and sings
Evening comes gradually at the end of the street

She walks and sings
Fragments of a tranquil song
break in my heart

Alas, the madness of tile and brick
Please sing and sing again
of all the destruction
you carry in your head

A PEACEFUL MADMAN

As he walks on the road
he stares with an ageless face
and unweathered body
Two eyes open two empty rooms

For a thousand steps he walks the same way
forgetting each step as he takes it
losing it behind him
He doesn't know where to take his next step

He walks and counts his steps on his fingers
counting to only one

In childhood we followed him laughing
As we grew
the sight of his shadow would interrupt our fun
and tease us into despair

Then he became more familiar
One day I happened to see myself
grumbling in a crowd

A RAINY NIGHT

To Thanh Thao

For a long time I haven't had a night like tonight
A random raindrop landing on my shoulder and neck
makes me remember roaming at night from Bac Qua flea market
to Hang Co train station
For one cent of *Ruou* I was able to fly to heaven
For the first time I secretly sold rice coupons
to buy loneliness on a street
Although thirty, I was still boyish
but became a man with a street prostitute
that nobody else desired

I looked for my fate in every distant place
in every kind of trouble
Being alive became just a habit
Tonight I'm in the South but feel the North's coldness
which makes me want a cup of black coffee
and draws me into the rainy night
on a motorcycle—not a bicycle, like those days
But I'm already fifty. How can I be with you again, old girl?

At thirty, I was a poet
Now I thirst for the lines of a poem
when this life turns me to stone
Suddenly I'm surprised by a single drop of rain

A MAN RETURNING HOME

He is home from *That*
His wife cries all night, his kids are confused all day
Home from *That*
when he walks through the door, his friends' faces are ashen
Home from *That*
he feels an itch on the back of his head
in the midst of a crowd
as if someone is watching

One year later, he suddenly chokes during a party
Two years later, he sweats from his nightmares
Three years later, he feels pity for a lizard
Years later, he has the habit of sitting alone in darkness

Some days, he feels a stranger's penetrating stare
Some nights, an aimless voice asks questions
He jumps
at a touch to his shoulder

BLACK DOG, BLACK NIGHT

For Nguyen Do

I

A dog
The black dog
The black dog runs into the night
warms the night with his snarling

II

The black dog barks at a blood-red jasmine

III

The black dog faces up, looking at the moon

IV

The black dog hisses in a complex code
Whose spirit is moving in the darkness tonight?

V

Oh, my dog, I'm so sad
Everyone forsakes me
Sniffing, he lays his mouth on my lips

VI

The black dog passionately searches all night long
An itch from his previous life
drives him crazy because he has no way to express it

A DOG OF STONE

Arriving at a village
I see a dog of stone

The stone dog sits in the river's stream incessantly
When will it cross over?

The stone dog wears out its eyes
The stone dog loses its face under cover of sadness

Returning to a previous life of stone
it stands like a small hill in the middle of a field

A boy raises his hand to ask it something
The stone dog laughs as it turns to powdered lime

AMERICA

I

For Paul Hoover

LAX was dark gray
The security man not as huge as I'd imagined
My luggage wasn't opened because a custom officer wanted to ask
   me about Vietnamese history
Sweaty, looking for another departure gate,
I was surprised to see Japanese plums blooming over the street

The Golden Gate stands up to the sky and turns a shade of red
The poet is peaceful and tall as a redwood tree

Waking in a glass-walled room
I lie there watching birds pick seeds from the garden
A flock of wild ducks swims freely on the pool
I miss so much my childhood that I'll never see again

At night, losing our direction in the puzzling darkness of a
   mountain road,
I suddenly see the *Ram* moon rising over San Francisco Bay

Where are the skyscrapers with colorful spinning lights, and where
   is the concrete, steely and ironic?
Only nature is forever secret
The deer shadows stupefied behind branches and leaves
The fallen redwood forest silent for thousands of years

II

For a Poet Friend

After four years without a trace
the moment we met it was like science fiction
One of us with a sidewalk fate; the other an escapee from his home
    country
We put our heads together in "heaven"
and laughed for a hundred miles as we sped down freeways

Fiction becomes the truth
because of poetry

Me listening to you brag
superciliously
and become aggressive
at a party
but
caring
persistent
When just you and me
run half of the earth's circle
you are still you

"Four years in the 'new economy' of America"
You show your chapped and scarred hands
"Never been refused any job that an immigrant has done"

How mournful but determined you are
me knowing that only poetry keeps you alive

Three days later
in that speeding car
both of these guys have red faces and pink ears as they argue about
   a poem
ready to say goodbye on the spot
Oh, poetry
What are you, poetry?

UNTITLED [WHERE DO THE STAIRS LEAD US]

Where do the stairs lead us?
The *bim* is purple; part of the brick wall shows through the stucco.
Where do the stairs lead us?
The coffee's smoke and a run-down shop.

The house fell long ago,
leaving only its stairs,
regretting the feet that had stepped up
and up.

Up to catch trails of white smoke.
Up to catch flocks of wild birds,
catch bewitchment, catch dizziness,
catch the rustling sound of the city's life.

The house fell long ago,
leaving only its stairs.

Where do the stairs lead us?
The foggy sky, no wings in flight.
The stairs suddenly come to a stop; the only way is back.

From the center of the street, a lonely kid is looking up.

UNTITLED [THE FAINT, DARK HALLWAYS]

The faint, dark hallways where you can only feel forward by
    touching.
The roads on which *co may* stitch themselves to your pant legs.
The distances of water echoing the sound of ducks' webbed feet.
The *H'mong* sky in which the leaves sing their nightly love songs.

Excited and anxious, your body is like a dancing flame.
Gentle and silent, you're a small-town girl with whispering
    eyesight.
You appear quickly, in sunlight from the sea, as the factory whistles
    a change of shift.
You are thirsty for love, your chest narrow and eyelids dark blue.
Why do you already rouge your lips too soon for your age?
Why do you look like the setting sun?
Why is your skin so damp and pale?
Your chest fully exhibits a lonely space.

FEVER

I flow, I swell to fill the space entirely.
I see myself flying up from the ground.
What is this fever that shocks the body, buzzing dizzily in my ears?

Your hands are like a cool creek
when I feel unsafe.

Quiet and distant as you read the sutra, your voice
comes from a previous life when we weren't yet devoted.
Your eyes are on the treetop
as you watch the train of life passing.
In this life I'm a clumsy devotee.
Have we had any other life, my dear?

It's shocking when the pillow gets wet
and my hands reach for you.
The lonely day gnaws its way toward night.
You sit like a mountain, in silent seclusion.
I'm still swaying, impermanent
because of the furious shaking under my skin.
When the fever releases,
I can be quiet, disperse into my words.

THE SMELL OF RAIN OR A POEM BELONGING TO M

The tears of humankind surround our house.
Lying down beside me, you tell a sad story
from deep in your heart, only now disclosed
like a suggestion from this amazing rain that no one has seen before.

For thousands of nights, rain makes the darkness white.
You miss my scent passionately, as a cow misses its excrement and
    garbage,
but I lost my scent from lying on strange floors.
All that remains is the smell of the rain, like the smell of fear at
    night.

Do you still love me, and how long will it last?
If you get angry and hate me, how long will it last?
For fifteen years, we haven't fully understood our own hearts.

Rain floods the first floor.
We climb to the top floor to listen to the rain
Pouring ironically on the roof
and wish, while listening, that we might die.

THE NIGHT OF CROSSING THE PASS

I close my eyes to complete the darkness.
The voice of the bus rages as it crawls over the pass.
With the sound of a wooden fish and the smell of sticks,
the coffin runs precariously.
My God, it's foggy—all direction is lost.
Where does the spirit go,
leaving a light in eternity
where every night you have prayed?

Nguyen Khoa Diem (1943–)

Nguyen Khoa Diem, born in the city of Hue, grew up in Hanoi and earned a degree in literature from Hanoi Pedagogic University before returning to his hometown in 1975. A former general secretary of the Vietnamese Writers Association and minister of the Department of Information and Culture, Nguyen Khoa Diem now works in Hanoi as a key leader of both government and the Vietnamese Communist Party. Winner in 2001 of the National Prize for Lifetime Contribution in Literature and in 1984 of the National Book of the Year Award for his poetry collection *The House with the Warm Flame,* Nguyen Khoa Diem has published ten volumes. His poetry surprises readers by means of what he calls his "poetry filter," which allows him to maintain verbal and emotional restraint regardless of the subject—even war or the difficult experiences of his own life. Unlike the typical "government poet," who writes predictably optimistic poems about Vietnamese society and politics, Nguyen Khoa Diem's poems are true to the given situation. At a time when few others had access to it, he worked in a modern idiom that is now considered classic.

MY MOTHER'S GARDEN

The vegetables are ready for harvest
My mother has been anticipating a gain from it
The ripening starts then stops
as the moon rises and the sun sets
We have grown up from our mother's hands,
the largest pumpkins and squashes growing down to grow larger,
like the shape of salty sweat drops
in the silent melody of her heart.
And we are the ones
our seventy-year-old mother still waits
to harvest
I get scared sometimes that our mother's hands will grow tired
while we are still so green!

THE HUONG GIANG EVENING

After this evening there may be others
Perhaps the clouds will be immense, perhaps the sunlight yellow
The wind blows these evenings along the riverbank
making everyone's hair look cool
This evening a cow steadily grazing
on the bank seems not to know the evening is gone
She and I share the silence of friendship
Her eyes look tenderly at the *Huong Giang* stream

Oh evenings, country home evenings
I have and haven't had!
Today at random in the late sunset
my eyes can still capture the crystal *Huong Giang*.

A COUNTRY PLACE

returning again, a crescent moon
in the endless sunset haze of the meadow
the frog's song broods in warm grass
rice is soft as a lover's shoulder

spring, this is the very spring
that releases birds in the perfumed grass of home
crossing an alley, a herd of buffalo with full bellies
drums their horns at the crescent moon

patiently waiting, a little nervous,
eighteen country girls
who miss their soldier boys very much
warm themselves with thoughts of them

then how strongly the wind blows
at the village well and riverbank
the pure singing of girls
rises like crystal toward the crescent moon

Tran Vu Mai (1944–1991)

After earning a BA in literature at Hanoi University in 1971, Tran Vu Mai volunteered to serve in the South as a journalist and writer during the American War. Early in his career, he wrote several poems and short stories with the ambition to be the Paul Éluard or Ernest Hemingway of Vietnam. Tran Vu Mai also published two book-length poems, "The Optimistic Sense" and "The Chim Lac Lady," as well as shorter poems about the wartime fate of the Vietnamese people. His poetry was influenced by the style of Tran Mai Ninh, who with Tran Dan first introduced the work of Mayakovsky to Vietnam during the war with France. Tran Vu Mai's poetry displays a vulnerability and purity of expression, evident in his works composed both during and after the war. Tragically, his life ended in suicide. In 1996, he was posthumously awarded the National Book of the Year Award for his collection *Poems and Long Poems*.

THE GRASSY BANKS OF HONG RIVER

This morning
your face is lost to me
I walk along the sidewalks looking for all our familiar distances
spotted with mosses and early light
their long, far curves
on which dark red firebricks dry in the sun

Here the rain has been falling
The sunlight is still sunlight
Like this green wall,
I know by heart the old signs of your passage

That was the night we walked under fire and cannons at Hong River
and in the rain and flood
Your hands were cold but not from fear
I thought tomorrow might resemble that cannon sky
and my face would catch fire
Please don't be absent tomorrow, my love,
your hands on the shoulders of soldiers,
which have become so strong since the war started
Tomorrow!

Hanoi will not be forgotten!
For the whole day, the sky seems very deep
I miss you, my love,
and everything I haven't shared with you
The marbled grass along the Hong River is so new!
Its greenness slopes down to say good-bye to me
If I found any fault in you, my love,
It's because I didn't want to find fault in myself
so I could stand face to face with you and smile naturally

and talk loudly as young people do
I will always be me

All that we have loved, dreamed, and been sad about
is covered in our hearts by Hong River grass
Now bombs and bullets fall on that mystery
and the devil's eyes have already stared at me!
I'm not the one at fault!
Don't be sad, my love
Whenever you are sad and feeling missed
I will feel the same and more
Small and white
you
stand on the grassy edge of the grassy bank of Hong River
extending a daisy
My love, don't be sad,
I'm only leaving for the "South Pole"!

THE GRIEVING SPRING

The spring's
fist is so hard
its slight wind stronger behind my head and back
Now that I'm an old man, how come I'm so silent?
My hands tremble turning page after page

The spring came early when I was seventeen
my hair silky with its parting
The first day of school was the first day of war, and the second day
   I was AWOL
Late at night I was heavy hearted to tell to my love good-bye
but no, it wasn't as heavy as the AK
I carried through battle fire
I left then returned
to my parents' home
My grandfather passed away
It's sad
When I realize yesterday was my birthday!

No longer dealing
with the reason that reason is gone
with a diary unsalted by tears
I sit down and my half-closed eyes seem less than human—
confused to be so distant
My footsteps are different, much slower than before

But my fists have become familiar
One is here, another there
Eight hours pass drowsily
Noisy? Noisy? Stay away!
I must seem haughty
sitting on the roof of a house as if in a chair

The night flashes don't scare me
An early death doesn't scare me
For a long time I haven't missed
my home

All right, get out of this nasty bog
but don't kiss a rolling train
Don't drink too much and talk too much
Don't commit adultery
Don't go too fast or too slow!

Looking up at the early stars of evening
I realize I've been avoiding a lot of nastiness and tears
I swear I won't try to be the kind of luck
that's not complicated, not pretend,
and, most important, not anesthetic
I swear I will find a changeling for my cancer
The moon is rising,
and the sun will rise, pleased to serve as witnesses

I have been wandering around
on feet of yellow fever,
of dioxin and blood,
of everything terrible that people have produced
Yes, before the doctors searched,
I searched passionately for this grieving spring

Y Nhi (1944–)

Born in Quang Nam Province, Y Nhi grew up in Hanoi; graduated from Hanoi University, where she studied literature; and lives in Ho Chi Minh City as a branch manager and editor of the Writers Association's publishing group. She was a journalist during the war and a member of the Vietnamese Writers Association. Y Nhi has published five poetry collections, including *A Woman Knitting*, which won the National Book of the Year Award in 1984. With Thanh Thao, Nguyen Duy, and others, she is associated with the Vietnam-American War period but has become better known as a postwar poet. She is one of very few female poets who have attracted the attention of readers by exploring the lives of women in Vietnam. Though very modern in tone and form, Y Nhi's poetry also exhibits the tenderness, silence, and sorrow of a woman who has experienced great loss in her life.

A WOMAN KNITTING

On a cold evening
a woman sits at a window and knits
patiently but quickly
Patience is like the work she must do in her life
Quickness is her last chance for happiness

No sigh
no smile
She keeps her pain a secret
her happiness also
Her heart is full of optimism
and doubt

Not once does she look up
She is either preparing for a first meeting
or living on after a last farewell
In the tips of her bamboo needles, what is hidden? Joyfulness
    or worry
in her eyes, exhaustion or expectation?

In the cold evening
the woman sits at a window and knits
Beneath her feet
a ball of wool like a blue globe
rolls slowly

SONG LYRIC

I am a *khuyen*
lying hidden in the woolen grass.
Its singing remains in your song.

I am a match
lying silently
in an ashtray.
Its fire flames in your fingers.

I am a boat
face down beneath a row of pines.
Its sea
flowed far away from you.

Always I am thrown back.
Always in my dream I see
the flame,
the singing,
and the sea.

MORNING

My darling, don't be sad.
The night did become morning.

Here's a cup of fresh water.
As I bring it to you,
Some of it overflows onto the wooden table.

Here's a ream of brand-new blank paper.
I set it on the table
In the hope that windows will open, one by one.

Here are my hands
Resting upon your hands: quiet
Loving words, forever attached.

My darling, please look—
A little bird returns once again,
Peacefully resting in an apricot tree.

A streak of sunlight is a deeper yellow on the grass path.
Don't be sad,
My love!
It was already sunrise.

EVENING

All sadness and happiness of the past
Are concentrated in this quiet evening.
A ray of sunlight in a treetop
Is enough to warm me this winter.

The evening settles like sand beneath a river's current,
Which worries as it runs continuously toward the sea.
Like ore that lies in the depths of a well,
Throughout the sunlight, there's the sound of wind.
Lyric songs are made pure by a loving heart.
Salt is still salty after thousands of years of waves crashing.

In moments of silence, there's no need for words.
Even if I had to speak, I wouldn't know what to say.
The shafts of sunlight behind the distant treetops
Are happy to be fire and also to be flame.

Thanh Thao (1946–)

A poet, sports reporter, and daily news columnist, Thanh Thao was born in Quang Ngai Province, grew up in Hanoi, took a degree in literature from Hanoi University, and now lives once more in Quang Ngai. He was a correspondent for Vietnamese Army Radio in the Southern campaign of the war with the United States. He became famous for his long antiwar poem "A Soldier Speaks of His Generation," which was sent directly from the heat of battle to his hometown newspaper in the North. He is a member of the Vietnamese Writers Association's poetry committee and president of its branch in Quang Ngai Province. Even though this position usually comes with Communist Party membership, he is not a member, the first such exception in history. Winner of the National Prize for a Lifetime Contribution in Literature in 2001 and two National Book of the Year Awards—for *The Footprints Passing a Meadow* in 1979 and the book-length poem *The Waves of the Sun* in 1996—he is one of the most popular contemporary poets in Vietnam. Both his poetry and lifestyle are very original, powerful, outspoken, and thoughtful. An admirer of the Russian poets Boris Pasternak and Sergei Essenin and the Spanish poet Federico García Lorca for the depth of their knowledge, Thanh Thao has successfully grafted the early modernist style of western lyric to his own. The publication of individual poems in the 1970s and his collection *The Rubik's Cube* in 1985 stunned the quiet world of Vietnamese poetry. Rich in thought and complicated in theme, Thanh Thao's poems also display a sense of humor, allowing readers to follow contemplation with laughter. Thanh Thao has published at least fifteen poetry collections and several other literary works.

SUDDENLY

suddenly
his face turned to the past
turned to a sigh
turned to hopelessness

suddenly
without apology
a man flew through the treetops
leaving behind a woman, a thin trail of smoke

suddenly
the ships searched for a place to rest
the stars searched for a place to be seen
crowding into a puddle of water
where it gives birth to the sky
suddenly
as the poems searched for their flames

comes a faint sound of women selling rice cakes
on my birthday
it makes me remember
a packet of rice
a bowl of dried sweet potato mixed with molasses
a mother thin as the morning light
and laughter beside a heap of trash

now I have become my thoughts
and love what I lack

on my birthday a boat floats to an empty space
a lonely street in which some leaves are rolling
a wood-burning stove is poked, its fire like a whisper,
echoes from fifty-six years ago
a day as pale as today
that no one cared about, no one remembered
a little puppy is dumbstruck looking at a lonely street

a boy with country blood was born in a town
in a quiet time before the storms and flames
it was a childhood rippling with dragonfly wings
and fireflies whispered at night
in front of the house, the river where I had swum since I was six
not with an otter's skill
but in the natural way of kids
to sink or to swim

2

Fifty-six stairs
some of them weepy and some with hiccups

I have almost forgotten them
like a fisherman whose nets are full

    3

how can I burn fifty-six candles
in the wind
if only in my life I could save a single one of them
but I blow them out instead
impossible!

ANDANTE FOR THE MILLENNIUM (2000)

I

When I circle myself
the way a dog marks its place by pissing,
that's when I break through,
because the high trees are calling,
the stars loudly call,
small bits of nothingness whisper,
a colorless beam of light
passes into my mind,
a woman pushes a trash can as if beating the drumhead of evening.
These are signs to me
to quickly clean up my mind,
be on time collecting the trash,
put the all away in the all,
to be perfectly clear.
That's the time,
as a star disappears,
when word after word appears.

II

The wind blew me
a sideways look.
I crouched like a mimosa
looking at its thorns
which are the tears of a tree
gazing at a dump where the moon is bright as milk.
A festival of dogs
barks at the moon and laughs.
They can smell tragedy,
call out with the same emotions

of those who search the night—
a job, a hope, a refuge,
an
  emptiness,
all that the dark night promises.

III

With two pens,
two chopsticks,
I'm going to look for the source of water
slowly and quietly.
Look, the pen is a little nervous,
breathing with every stroke.
I know I'm in a drought;
go slowly and silently.

IV

When I was young,
I spent my time like rain sinking into sand.
Now I add leaf to leaf
on the branch,
save a box of matches to keep warm in winter.
The old box can't be recognized by its cover.
In childhood I held a black cricket.
Now at five in the morning, a kid is learning to walk on crutches,
a truck vomits black smog into the new millennium,
a mentally ill woman with amnesia runs beneath a street light,
and behind the sunrise
the mayflies cease for a moment
all their searching and finding.

V

I already know
that other worlds
are no different—
a bird that tries to love its cage
has no need to begin singing.

UNTITLED [UP AND DOWN A FISHING ROD]

Up and down a fishing rod
to fish dreams of the past,
the dreams
of snatching shadows from under the green sadness
of water hyacinths.
I come again to my father and mother's home
where a newly planted yellow plum suddenly blooms
like a spotlight on a flood plain,
like my mother's eyes
staring from the garden's corner
where custard apple has a pure greenness.
I come again
to the well,
its perfectly rounded sky,
and the tree's oblique shadow
like my mother's shape,
the faint sound of bells
and the rainy bells of the leaves
twinkling as they watch me;
childhood's crystalline cloud
drifts.
I'm silent as a coconut palm
that doesn't know why it bore fruit!

THE FIRE

Your spirit is like a slowly blooming flower
ecstatic, I choke with emotion
returning lonely to my home at night
I myself catch the firelight
for a long time
the petals are tightly closed
in boring
forgettable
misery
please let me thank the convent
where the votive fire burns continually
where I exhausted myself in praise of you
and my body scattered in the deepest part of the night
for a long time
your convent flower
flares like a spirit

TO SUDDENLY REMEMBER

like someone beating a drum, the rain dropped on my waterproof
    army poncho
which was torn and badly needed mending
my friends were like forest trees, day by day diminishing
the war cut them down
like an electric trimmer
but now they're all at peace
I remember also that evening, as a child,
the sweetness of the banana in my mother's hand,
even sweeter when she carried me on her back!
the road over the dike echoed the soul of the river
dark brown sails and bamboo shadows floating slowly
a bridge where an older man got tired
and lay down to rest but not sleep
the room where he keeps only the barest necessities
the ripe smell of bananas
some old chairs
and a small ancient teapot
the aged sunlight
an evening of summer rain
and the bombs' echoes from the Duong bridge that sounded like
    rolling thunder
my parents lived there in a home
a ten-square-meter country
but because of our greater home
my parents didn't prevent me
from going into battle
not hoping for a brave death or "rainbow"
I'm the hand on a compass
that only turns toward our room
where everything is old

MIMI

I

I saw you, Mi, run around the moon's back
barking
you were the best of dogs
you could outbark all the shadows
had footsteps like clouds
you still console me on the hottest of days

II

when someone loudly calls my name
I always depend on your eyes
which were brown as the earth

III

when the wind was gathering wave after wave
and the light of sunrise waved up and down
you flew past on four feet
in a good mood on a sad day
your ears twitched gently toward darkness

IV

haven't seen you on a staircase
haven't seen you in the air
our home was suddenly vast
with the faintest sound of your steps
you moved through the walls

V

your muzzle rubs against my heart
the night bursts into tears

A LEAF

someday
a green tree will hand me a leaf
inscribed with unclear words
as we are closely related
lonely and silent at night
miserable by day
it will have something it wants to say
someday

WAVE OSCILLATION

I

Following me are sad dreams
in which my dying mother's face appears,
like nights of worry as the rough sea drones.
Mother, so lovely, where did you vanish?
How do I turn time back to the past? How?

II

For all of my life, two shade trees have consoled me.
Whose footsteps remain
on the village trail?
What lights are in your eyes now that the rain has cleared?
Now the small stain of a star rises deeply,
a horizontal line that separates two sufferings,
but still leaves the spicy, fragrant smoke of our stove
in the garden with its dark green banana leaves—
from morning to night you still walk back and forth there!

AND YOU WAKE ME UP, GINSBERG . . .

And you wake me up, Ginsberg, where I sleep on a log like a dog that sometimes speaks in sleeping, waves its tail and howls with smoldering anger. And you wake me up with an owl in front of a forest, a drop of morning haze, the sound of a person on the street recovering his previous life, the wind shredding newspapers, the short lives of a series of drafts extolling the mass media, and a bicycle rolling and flickering on a hot day. And you wake up me, a suppressed kid, a miserable, homeless man; all untruths are listed under my name; my success and prosperity are confirmed, recycled most likely from waste. But no one can recycle the pain and tears, although they want to create literature. You wake me up as roughly as a cop rouses a beggar dreaming on a park bench, rubbing his eyes as he thinks about dreaming another dream. The paths I have been walking, both long and short, are meaningless; however, I wait and, while waiting, I sink into the newspapers, throwing word after word, all those miserable words, in exchange for a few pennies by the never-green leaves. This summer is so hot; I'm really tired. But you wake me up, Ginsberg, I stand up as the morning rises, a howling rises, the green of never-green leaves rises. We live without limits, but who knows what is best to do in these heavy times. The howling in blood, the rebel cells, isn't strong enough to become a tumor, but it doesn't matter. I know someone who gives people immortality pills or secretly puts mines of expectation in their chests; they will make this world shiver before it sinks again in their sleep. Their mission is like a fly in a bowl of soup. I'm sick; please turn the sunlight blue until it's salvation. You wake me up in time, which the sun confirms by raising its hands in my direction. And now I'm as immovable as a dusty plastic sunflower.

THIS IS USUAL

You tell me that I'm melancholy, but what the hell is it if I'm
　　healthy as you, and what's the source of your power?
In a rainstorm we hear the sound of sighing—we can't say what we
　　think or try to say what we don't know.

The river is as puzzling as breath; it decorates its voice.
You don't talk, but the way you are silent speaks more than
　　speaking.
I have experienced many holes, many rains, which crash into the
　　shade through leaves and branches,
which are in shock.
I lean on time to catch the time that doesn't run out.
To ignore the land is to be old, dry, lean, and thirsty.
You persuade me by lying down in my cocoon then searching for a
　　way home, looking calmly at a catfish that gives birth at the top
　　of a banyan tree
in the summer-fool-crazy rainstorm.

A JOURNEY

A daydream takes me; I go into the private darkness of light.
The darkness differs significantly from reality, but it is still the
    reality
of a cow chewing the sunset; on one side is the yellow sunrise,
    on the other the darkness of sunset—
the faint border between
reunion, separation, reunion.
We have lived by suddenly moving, freely and easily, from
    one area to another.
The lonely one who travels only with his mind
on unending hallways
to meet relatives who passed away
is as happy as any tourist
with blocked views.

Please,
don't dig any holes that will break my journey!

THE GOAL

A truck. The dark, nasty night. Losing direction. Trying to climb down in order to climb up. Can't see that truck. Can't see the way home. Fences. Strangers. Another truck. But not the one I was looking for. That's probably *Truong Son*. There must be another war. But no. The truck. My "brother" the driver vanishes. I'm suddenly very confused. Can't see the goal. Where do I go? The night is like a cocoon. Pictures flicker. There are human beings, but I'm unable to speak to them. No way home. No address. A stair slopes increasingly up. Slipping. Down is easier than up. Slipping down then vanishing. Trying to talk louder by remaining quiet. Trying to speak without a sound. All that remains are the views skimming along in the side mirror.

Drawing the bow intensely then suddenly releasing. No arrow. But feeling little pain. Maybe the arrow secretly shot back, but I don't know. Sometimes I choke when I swallow something. Don't know where it runs to. A heat between my chest and my belly. I have been neither waiting nor expecting very much. But how come that arrow still comes back? The darkness flows into secret corners. I crouch like a rock or root. Someone sits on me, mumbles and spits, then leaves. The night gnashes and grinds. I don't want to be alone, to be the bare branch waving alone, like a cow or buffalo waves its tail. I want to say something for someone. But no one is here, or they are here but I didn't know. Don't know what to say. Everyone counts their steps on their own separate path. The sound of counting makes it into a path. I don't know how to count or I count wrong. Do I have no path? Here are the breaking lines on the dike where my self is flooding. Why do I stand on the bank of my river life, frightened to jump into it, even just to get wet? Who doesn't dare to swim doesn't dare to sink!

A SOLDIER SPEAKS OF HIS GENERATION

The day we leave,
    the doors of the passenger train open wide.
There's no longer a reason for secrets.
The soldiers, young as bamboo shoots,
      playfully stick their heads from the windows.
The soldiers, young as bamboo shoots,
     in too-big uniforms,
crowd together like tree leaves on the stairs between cars.
The train whistles too loudly
And too long, as if broken,
like the voice of a boy who nearly has his man's voice now.

In our generation,
that train whistle is a declaration.

The generation in which each day is a battle,
its mission heavier than the barrel of mortar 82
that we carry on our shoulders.
The generation that never sleeps,
that goes half naked and patiently digs trenches,
that is naked and calm in its thinking,
that goes on its way as the past generation has gone,
by ways various and new.

In the forest, names are quickly engraved on trees.
Their canteens are engraved with the letters *N* and *T.*
Each backpack contains a uniform,
some dried fish sauce, and a small lump of steamed rice.
The camp's woodstoves flame on the stone bank of a creek,
above which hang tall cans of sour soup
made from *Giang* leaves and shrimp sauce.

What we have,
    we share,
        share on the ground
            completely.
To enemies, we spend all we have in battle.
To friends, we give until all we have is gone.

If you see that our skins are black from the sun,
our misshapen bodies seem older than they are,
and you can count the calluses on our hands
along with the war medals—still, nothing quite describes us.

Oh, the clearing in *Dau* forest with its dry, curved leaves!
Every footstep crackles like a human voice.
In the night as we march,
several fires suddenly flare on the trail,
our generation with fire in our hearts
to light the way to our goal.

One night when rain lashes on all four sides,
we're in *Thap Muoi* with no tree to hide us.
As the swamp floods, we have to push our boats against the rising tide.
The horizon lies behind whoever drags himself ahead,
silhouetted by the flash of lightning.

Our generation has never slept, walks every night in the flood.
Mud covers us thickly from head to foot.

So our voices are those of cowboys,
and our gazes are sharp as a thorn,
because the fire that can burn in a bog is the true fire.
When it flames up,
it burns with all of its strength.

What do you want to tell me in the hazy night, *Quoc,*
as you sing passionately all through the flood season?
The *Dien Dien* flower raises its hot yellow petals
like the face of a hand that sunlight lands and stays on.
Our country comes from our hearts, simply,
like this *Thap Muoi* that needs no further decoration
                              and is completely silent.
Stronger than any romance, this love goes directly
to any person
who doesn't care about the limits of language.

Unexpectedly, I meet my close friend again.
We both lie down on a *My Long* trail,
on an army coat under the dark sky,
where just this evening a B-52 harrowed the earth three times,
where for several years the bomb craters are uncountable,
where I suddenly speak a simple dream:
"When peace truly comes,
I will go to trail number four, spread out a coat and lie down
        completely satisfied."
My friend gazes
at a star rising from a water-filled crater.
His eyes look so strange; I see
they contain both the star and the crater. . . .

A vortex spins on the roof of an ancient forest.
The wind whistles a long time inside the empty shells of trees.
The bats flicker in and out of sight.
A flattened place in the cane grass smolders.

We have passed the limits of the dry season,
passed the rainy season, the long limits of the rainy season
when every night our soaked hammocks hang on *Tram* poles.

Our boats move across the river under the faint flares of the
    American army.
Sometimes, in awe of the skyline filled with red clouds at evening,
we forget we are older than we are.
Our feet walk in rubber sandals across a hundred mountains,
but our shadows never walk ahead of our futures.

Past battles come again in memory.
Rockets explode against the sky in a mass of smoke.
Our hearts beat nervously in our very first fight.
Our army-issue canteens smell as they burn
        on the roofs of the trenches.
And the garbage cans lie strewn all around.
In the silence and deafness between two bombings,
a hen's voice suddenly calls
from a small, ruined canal.

Our generation has never lived on memory
so we don't rely on the past's radiance.
Our souls are fresh as *Chuong* wind,
our sky the pure blue of a sunlit day.

The transport boats sail the crowded *Bang Lang* canal.
That evening rockets attack,
bending down the *Binh Bat* trees.
Sunset covers both banks like blood.
The canal turns white from the flow of toxic gases.
Suddenly I see my face on the water's surface,
among those poisonous mists,
on which floats the *Binh Bat* fruit,
on which floats our breaking country,
and I see
also floating the faces of many people,

some of them friends and some I have never seen.
They are so very young
as they flicker along on the stream
into a distant meadow
            on an endless evening.

They're the people who fought here first,
twenty years ago as one generation,
and also the ones who will come later,
twenty years from today.

That evening
on the small canal
artillery attacks and flowing water.
How clearly you can see
        the faces of
                our generation!

Nguyen Duy (1947–)

A poet and journalist, Nguyen Duy lives in Ho Chi Minh City, where he works as a branch manager, editor, and staff writer for a literary review. Author of at least ten poetry collections, he won the National Book of the Year Award in 1984 for *The Moonlight*. Nguyen Duy was born in Thanh Hoa Province, graduated from Hanoi University with a degree in literature, then served as an army engineer who fought face to face with US troops. After the war, he became a member of the Vietnamese Writers Association. He is also an inter-chapter party secretary of the United Association of Vietnamese Art and Literature. In the late 1980s, everyone in Vietnam was familiar with his poem "Looking Home from Far Away," which confronted current political and moral issues in the country. At the time, due to the Renovation Movement related to the tearing down of the Berlin Wall, his theme was a sensitive one. However, what most defines Nguyen Duy's work is his beautiful use of the traditional Vietnamese idiom, an influence that derives from the folk poet Nguyen Binh (1919–1969), who worked in traditional forms. Nguyen Duy's poetry is known less for its refinement of feeling and more for its humor than the work of Nguyen Binh; however, both are "bestsellers" among Vietnamese poets.

DALAT—ONCE WITH THE MOON

A magical moon flickers in white fog
Whose wind flickers over the hills?
The crunching sound of a horse's hooves beating on the silent slope
A pine leaf faintly and dimly falls

You light a camp stove with scraps of dry wood
The flame covers the emptiness between you and me
I avoid looking at you; you avoid looking at me
while our little teapot mumbles as it boils

But finally nothing is avoided
In their heart these wooden coals burn at their reddest
But their flame pretends to glimmer
and the odor of sap follows the drifting smoke

SITTING IN SADNESS, MISSING MY MOTHER . . .

The odor of *hue* perfumes the night sorrowfully
Smoke from incense draws the path passing into Nirvana
Sticks of incense are heaped by their ashes
as when long ago my mother's shadow walked and walked in a hurry

My mother didn't have a scarlet *yem*
and *quai thao* hat, but a simple *me*
One hand on her pumpkin-daughters, the other on her squash-sons,
for four seasons, her skirt was dyed by mud and her shirt stained
    brown

White crane, harsh sycamore sour peach
The wind has already carried to heaven that folk song she sang
Even when I go entirely to my fate
I will never equal that simple lullaby

When the autumn approaches
persimmon and grapefruit hang and swing in the *Ram*
When May approaches
my mother spreads a rush mat for me to lie on to count the stars

The galaxy flows across the sky
As it swings, the areca-sheath fan fitfully hums a song of *Thang Bom*
Fireflies flicker at the edge of the pond
making a sweet melancholy of long-ago happiness and sadness

My mother sang the truth of life
Milk builds the body but song builds the soul
The grandmother lullabies the mother, and the mother lullabied me
Will my children remember that?

Looking back to my mother's home village far away
my heart is as moist as the place she lay down on rainy nights
Sitting in sadness, I miss my mother
Her mouth chewing steamed rice
her tongue picking bones from fish to feed me

DO LEN

In my childhood I went to Na bridge to fish
clung to my grandmother's skirt on the way to the Binh Lam flea
     market
caught sparrows in the ears of Buddhist sculptures
and sometimes stole eye-dragon fruit at the Tran pagoda

In my childhood, I played in the Cay Thi temple
and walked barefoot in darkness to watch the Song temple's
     ceremony
The odor of white lily mixed with aloewood smoke was delicious
The sorceress's shadow staggered in the *van* melody

I didn't realize how miserable my grandmother was
She groped for crabs and skimmed for shrimps at Dong Quan
She carried green tea leaves to sell at Ba Trai,
Quan Chao, and Dong Giao; her shadow tottered on cold nights

I was solid crystal between the real and unreal,
my grandmother and the fairies, Buddhists and saints
These were starving years, the *dong* boiled but not yet done
Why did its smell seem like white lily and aloewood perfume?

America bombed; my grandmother's house blew away
Song temple exploded, blowing down other temples and pagodas
Saints and Buddhists were committed to leaving together
My grandmother went to sell eggs at Len train station

I had been in the army a long time and never returned to my
     grandmother's home
As one riverbank increases, the other decreases
When I realized I loved her, it was too late
My grandmother now lies in a grass-covered grave!

LOOKING HOME FROM FAR AWAY

Facing the light,
the bright blank paper seems to be made of it.

The North Pole's white night turns around frightened
as someone crouches, staring behind me.

Talking to myself makes me calm enough to look at my home
    country—
faraway, silent,
its mountains and rivers
and cracks in the earth.

Closing my eyes to see
deeply
with love and pain
I writhe like the hero in a tragedy.

Wherever I am, my home country is always in my heart.
Its borders stretch from missing to loving.

   *
* *

The light is so bright it overheats my eyes.
Someone flickers behind me like a ghost.
Who?
Silently!
Who?
The shadow!
Ah . . .
Hello to the tall, powerless hero,
the long black one lying on the floor.

OK, me, it's back to me again,
talking with my bloody shadow.

          *
      *   *

Once we loved to sing in chorus
heartily and with feeling:
"We are only ourselves, but we are passionate."
Yes! Once there was a huge period
of huge painfulness, hugely bloody.
The eyes of death open with a glare and don't want to close.

Yes. That was the time when we could reject nothing;
all had to flow in only one direction, no contrasting flow allowed.
False idols sputtered like green onion in boiling oil, frying spoiled
     food
that made me sick in the stomach and the heart.

          *
      *   *

We made it through the war,
but the torment was like a sore on our heel
that pained us with every step.
The war is over now, but it still feels present.
Our country is rich, so why are we rich in homelessness?

Who?
No one.
The dark shadow punches itself in the chest

          *
      *   *

A kind country,
but why do so many disabled soldiers make their living illegally?
Crutches pockmark the village trails.

The mothers of the honored dead call their sons to open their
    graves and carry their own corpses,
to sue the headless ghosts, to set up ambush around the homes of
    the powerful.

Who?
No one.
The dark shadow weakly extends its hands.

    *
 * *

A charitable country, but why are there so many ghosts—
devils-pimps-police-slyness . . .
And incarnate evils with their leaning shadows?

Secret night.
The hair on the back of my head seems to be rising, and my heart
    is nothingness
with bright blue eyes.

Who?
No one.
The dark shadow looks up at the sky.

    *
 * *

A miraculous country,
but why do so many temples and churches become warehouses for
    corporations
making plans to cheat even God

The paper is torn, but don't save its edge.
The Buddha statues weep; belief has disappeared.
Good and Evil can't be distinguished.
Justice drains away.

Who?
No one.
The dark shadow sits in contemplation.

　　*
　*　*

A talented country,
but why are so many children illiterate
and the schools so shabby?
Childhood stoops its shoulders beneath its sweat and tears.
Childhood bends its back to make money refilling bicycle tires.
Childhood's fate blows like leaves across the road.
"Blind eyes catch the goat" wherever people meet our talented children,
but opening their eyes . . . those talented shadows look like the
　　homeless.

Who?
No one.
The dark shadow silently bows its head.

　　*
　*　*

A trustworthy country,
but why are there so many hookers—
hookers in mansions, flea market hookers, and hookers on the
　　farm . . .
The low ones sell their vaginas to fill their mouths.
The high ones sell their mouths to fill their vaginas.
The cost of products goes up,
the soul's price goes down.

Who?
No one.
The dark shadow scratches its ears.

　　*
　*　*

A hardworking country,
but why so much laziness,
skilled people unwilling to work,
pretending they're receiving checks,
pretending to be at work,
not caring about their crimes
and ignoring the crimes of others?
Thieving is like a religion.
Illegal enterprises parade down the road,
trading everything, including saints and jobs.
Jobs are auctioned by the courts.

Who?
No one.
The dark shadow shrugs.

*
* *

A forgiving country,
but why do so many people leave their homes?
So many good-byes, but they're still smiling broadly,
ignoring their rice fields, careless as widows,
crowding the ports to work in foreign countries.
Boats filled with fate float on the Pacific Ocean.
They close their eyes with each step forward, no promise of
    returning home.

Who?
No one.
The dark shadow tears out its hair.

*
* *

A disciplined country,
but why are there so many kings

of illegal business—swindling king, mugging king,
the king without a throne, medium king, little king . . .
Landlord and warlord join forces.
Bullies swarm together, their faces like horses and buffaloes.
The law is simply a joke, sometime yes, sometimes no.
One person walks like a crowd along the people's path.

Who?
No one.
The dark shadow folds its ruler.

*
* *

?
?
?

*
* *

Who?
Who?
Who?
No one.
I ask myself, so tired.
The dark shadow bends its back like a question mark.

*
* *

That's all, I'm going home
with all the blank paper left, because it's virgin
and still glimmers in my heart.

*
* *

Sometimes blazing up, as if in a trance,
Spirit rushes from my body.

It plucks out my intestines and liver to count them,
pricks a drop of blood for a diagnostic test.
In me are an intellectual, a farmer, a hooker,
a businessman, a government employee, a joker,
a Buddhist and a ghost, all related to each other, if only a little.
Each makes the others miserable
because it's hard to remove so many masks.
Let's take them off now, no more delay.
You've been lying, but you can't much longer.
Being smart and stupid both have a limit.

*
* *

Something's wrong. It makes me nervous.
The "food" of transition has been swallowed too quickly. It's raw,
unclean, and, because of our pride, indigestible.
The unconscious knows the truth—people are glad to be poisoned.
For a long time, diseases and defects have lain in wait.
We knew it all along, but have no cure.
Maybe a "cursing pill,"
but the cursing leaders will use it to bare their teeth to even more
    opportunity!
Maybe a pill of dry grass chewed by a cow.
But let's pray to a machine, dear Sir and Madam.
Let's give up on bird songs.
Don't sound so loud and conceited while people are starving and sick,
And those who bend their backs while working for others stand
    straight while eating.
Is it true "renovation," or are we just pretending?
Can we replace blood when we have blood poisoning?

*
* *

It's scary having no one to love,
but so much scarier if there's no one to hate.

Day after day, we rarely write poems from our hearts and blood.
Who are we?
Do we need to be needed? By whom?

*
* *

Maybe we don't trust someone,
Maybe someone doesn't trust us.
But we still trust what's human.
Don't fold your arms in resignation.
How tragic to huddle together, averting your faces.
The good is much greater than the bad, so why is the bad stronger?
The good must join together.

*
* *

But the country is still in the heart.
The spirit streams are fresh.
Poetry is still alive, but will the people survive?
They are me, so it's me who exists.

*
* *

Drop after drop,
tough and heavy,
how tough and heavy.

In spite of that,
don't sigh.
"Having skin will grow the hair—having roots will grow a tree."

Nguyen Quang Thieu (1957–)

Nguyen Quang Thieu, author of five poetry collections, is one of the best Vietnamese poets whose work has been translated to English. Born in Ha Tay, he is a former police officer and now lives in Hanoi, where he works as an editor for the literary review *Van Nghe* and serves as a member of the Vietnamese Writers Association. He won the National Book of the Year Award in 1994 for his poetry collection *The Sleeplessness of the Flame*. Giving beautiful and original expression to traditional Vietnamese views, Nguyen Quang Thieu's poetry became a model for some young Vietnamese poets of the later 1990s. Influenced by Pablo Neruda and other Latin American poets whose work he read while studying in Cuba, Nguyen Quang Thieu's poetry contains classical themes and movements as well as more modest observations of the everyday. While his subject matter is consistent, his sense of structure changes from work to work. Nguyen Quang Thieu's poems possess a transforming power, an undercurrent of strangeness rooted in the life of his native region.

THE SPIRITS OF COWS

Departing at night,
now in darkness the shadow cows come
to the last meadow.

All night, the lowing of the herd
rises plaintively over the silent meadows.
All night, the breathing of the herd
blows hot as a summer night.

They have plowed their last row.
Their yokes are removed early in the morning.
Their hooves are already imprinted
on all the world's meadows.

In the morning, the herd grows more and more golden
then vanishes into sunlight.
Its lowing is echoed
in the trumpet concert of a small Christian village,
where people practice one last time
for the Eastern ceremony.

Now there are only masses of clouds,
the shapes of cows
flying over the meadows
which belong to other cows.

WOMEN CARRYING RIVER WATER

Long, black, and bony, their toenails splay wide as a hen's.
For five years, fifteen years—thirsty years and half my life—
I've seen them carry water from the river.
Their hair flows down their soft, wet backs,
one hand supporting the thin shoulder poles,
the other clinging to the whiteness of clouds.
The river hides its face in its banks then turns and runs on.
The men leave home silently, carrying fishing poles and dreams
    of the ocean.
The spiritual fish turn their faces away to weep.
Buoys made of corn sink in the river's flow.
Angrily and sadly, men are leaving the home
that I have seen for five years, fifteen years—thirsty years and half
    my life—
following these women who carry river water like naked children
who run along with their mothers and soon grow up.
The girls will always lay poles on their shoulders and go to the shore.
The boys will always leave home silently, carrying fishing poles and
    ocean dreams.
And the spiritual fish will always turn their faces to weep
in front of the bait, dumbstruck as it gazes from its fishhook.

EXCHANGING STARS

The landing at the head of the stairs is always covered by darkness
I have stopped there and opened my eyes wide
but never seen clearly whose faces
are barely saying hello, their small moans before disappearing
as if the hand of the Grim Reaper were erasing all traces

Where sometimes I meet my girl
but we can't identify each other
We both run away, afraid
that someone can see us standing close in darkness

Where in a small world of shadows
Both the blind and not blind
Climb slowly step after step
But no one offers a light

And I have seen
children yelling loudly
as they run upstairs quickly
and stars exchange places in the dark sky.

Nguyen Do (1959–)

A poet, journalist, and translator, Nguyen Do was born in Ha Tinh Province and moved to Hanoi as a youth. After taking degrees in surveying from Hanoi Construction College and in literature from Vinh University, Nguyen Do lived for many years in Ho Chi Minh City, where he worked as an editor and reporter for a literary review and other newspapers and magazines before moving to the United States to study English. Nguyen Do is a special case in Vietnam, both in his life and poetry. When his first poems were published in newspapers and literary reviews, some wondered why they were so sad and criticized them as too personal. Ignoring this criticism, Nguyen Do continued to write under the influence of Western literature and culture. As a result, his poetry collections, *The Fish Wharf and The Autumn Evening* (1988, in collaboration with Thanh Thao) and *The Empty Space* (1991), are among the most painfully lonely books published at that time. Nguyen Do is one of few Vietnamese poets to write about the existential loneliness of city life; he does so with an intensity that sometimes borders on insanity and nihilism. While living in Vietnam, he wrote many articles criticizing the government and legal system. As a result, for eight years nothing he wrote could be published under his name. He earned a living by publishing sports and arts reporting under a dozen different pseudonyms. He is not a member of the Vietnamese Writers Association. In 2005, he received a grant from The Fund for Poetry.

THE LIGHT

the pain appeared late at night
with its odor of acrid perfume
even my fingers seemed to be lost

in the morning I woke up
and had just one more drink
tonight I'm touching myself
as one slowly climbs a hill

"gently, please"
footsteps from two years ago just flew by
and three days in a row the sun didn't come up

the zipper of my memory is closing
your nipple is suddenly bright

HEADACHE

suddenly I'm like a helpless goalkeeper
dumbstruck looking at the empty space beneath the players' bodies

clasped hands on my ass walking out of a blind alley,
I'm the same, a rat sticking out of a hole

punching the back of my head I see
flamboyance blossom but not redness

one step ahead is a newsstand
another step is a country liquor store run by a dwarf
tomorrow I have to give you a new broom
why don't people say anything?

I place my hands on my head and press it to the ground
it becomes dark and sweaty
I'm scared to look at you
you smile so nakedly

I will give you a bowl of vegetable noodle soup
although it belongs in the trash, it has a sweet scent
darkness illuminates darkness

MEMORY OF A DAY

eight hours a day my only duty
is talking softly to myself, "take it slow and easy,"
and sometimes I get it right

I drop by a pharmacy to buy some aspirin
and jump onto the scale
yesterday it was up two pounds, today down one
I saved fifty cents by buying the medicine, too

the last scorching beam of day chases my family out of a tree house
the house is full of mystery and the stresses of the day
as a ball rolls out of its net
as we back slowly into the darkness, we seem happy to argue together

we have to be there anyway
anyway it has to be
talking with a deaf person is better than speaking with just anyone
who has a funeral for a dead tree?
a thousand Beethovens stand along the highway

MORNING

every morning my heart beats nervously
when I look up at the sky, where a dead leaf is hanging
I don't go out on the street
my chair is my boundary

hugs from people are like the bars of criminal courts
the crescent moon hides its full flame
a cigarette burns in an alarming way
only the darkness is safe and the bed is tender

don't go out on the street
three roses surprisingly committed suicide
light is the color of bread
just like the faces of those who've betrayed me

A SYMPHONY OF FRIENDSHIP

is it possible to return to an old blind alley
full of nasty eyes?
I launch into questions in a darkness that's five below
then call myself at my old phone number
011
848
8299221
and listen to its lonely, hoarse voice scream continuously
my heart is so painful it seems to be choking

my memories are like a door falling off its hinges
old, broken, but full of love
I'm scared to put it back together
because it opened and closed my life

nowadays I fall to pieces easier than the kids
I sit feeling sorry that I couldn't bring with me
the phone's voice and an old tattered shirt
shirts and other garments have their own fates

writing "done" above each sentence I suddenly remember
a small, likeable poem of an old friend
every thing has its own karma, everything
so
a song of sounds ceasing
is more interesting and lives longer than the original itself

and me?

my lovely friends
I'm not a Tagore or Whitman

or Ginsberg writing to praise you
I'm Do, a skinny illness
but I swear I won't be less than you without sorrow
the canegrass hair of my fate will be gray as you are

living miserably on the way to my goal
lacking fresh air and the cheerful, particular perfume of your faces
I'm dropping a long rope down my life-well
to fish out your shining glances
which would never be there if the well were dry!

FOR MY LOVELY AU

your light always contains my light
lonely, shy, careless, and full of adventure
not a single skip-rope circle welcomes you
not a single tree branch offers a leaf to protect you from sunlight
you have to pick one for yourself

I love to watch you eat or walk upstairs singing
when you were born forty years ago
the sweetest of folk songs appeared
sweet as the milky grains of young girl rice raised in a *Lao* wind
and people who see their faces in gravel on Lonely Hill after a
     rainstorm
the eternal faces of banyan tree roots on the banks of La River
the faces of your grandparents
the faces of everyone

I wish someday
that as the night passes, as the river whispers and falls asleep in the
     moonlight
I could cry once more as I listened to your singing!

MISSION

hearing the wind whisper and the dew call my name
I ride my bike down the street at noon, smiling like crazy
I always go too fast—sorry!
I promise to write a letter this evening

alone at night, growing smaller and smaller
and frightened, I bite my wife's feet
thirteen alleys, thirteen cups of coffee
thirteen successful missions
all ending in fire and the odor of smoke

every day I try to push myself
closer to the bead of a rifle
in order to become its favorite target

UNTITLED [FEELING EXTREMELY SAD]

feeling extremely sad
I'm face to face with the bottom of an empty beer bottle
thought jacks off but never quite thinks

I'm as exhausted
as the last losing player on the field at the end of the game
even the boos are gone
it's shocking to realize I'm actually having a nightmare in a movie
    theater
nasty chairs with black eyes stare straight through me

where are the kisses of our miserable adventure
the time we were together like pumpkins, squashes, and zucchinis
laughing as we dropped our shorts
where is the darkness of winter nights, black as the bottoms of old
    clay pots
emitting a perfume of mystery, worry, and hope

now I'm face to face with you
the bottoms of our clothes
explode away from us

THE UNLUCKY DAYS

To Thanh Thao

this evening I want to hug the trees on my street
but not because of their courage
I want to embrace my typewriter
the keypads that whisper to me

my home is on the blind alley of a lonely street
all year long only a few bohemian faces appear on its veranda
I rely on the sound of their footsteps

the sad songs no longer make me sad
the cat pissing on my desk doesn't bother me any more
the little pine tree is suddenly half-dead
it laughs at me while I chase a rat

I'm half-naked walking into the street
suddenly I remember the name of a person
who was not my friend and died a long time ago. . . .

THEME I

Have you ever told a stranger, "I'm so sad"?
On an evening out with five million people, with a wife, a daughter,
and no hunger? On the smoothest of avenues, I did. . . .
Luckily, he was polite and gently nodded.
Seeing the branch of a tree, dry and crooked, on a sidewalk at
  midnight,
I quickly bent down to touch it.

I try to persuade a dog, whom I pass on the street everyday, that he
  mustn't bark so loudly.
Sometimes I wave him along or offer my voice, a soft and lovely
  harmony.
Only once did he let me touch him gently on the head.
Today, however, he sings a long bark-song.
Is it possible to tell him of my melancholy?

I can't remember how many times in my thirty-seven years
I've barked to you on the phone.
So I am content to make a few passersby pay attention
(among seventy million hopefuls)
by barking and barking.

A LYRIC SONG FOR NGOC

There is something in the maple's spirit,
the goldenness and sincerity of consolation,
as if it's the last piano concerto of its life,
swaying slightly and sighing.

The doctor with the gray–white hair smiles softly
above a dark, blood-clotted wound.
The pale gray sky resembles my mother's voice—
"*au o* . . the cane fell asleep on its one foot."

Am I the cane that lands on that maple,
or the note in which Beethoven suddenly feels pity,
or nothing,
just a back all covered with cuts and bruises?

SILLINESS

Every night I wind the alarm clock's spring
as if shyly pretending to yawn among strangers,
removing a leaf of grass
and inserting it into a dark hole which it has never seen.

Never been . . .
When leaving my home, I often wish
somewhat
if there is a somewhat.

I usually wake up early, at three in the morning
daring to face the twinkling of the invisible,
while my partner smiles in her dream.
I step on a cat curled behind the door.

I think
all things know how to breathe and be sad.
In brief, they understand it all.

WITH . . .

I'm a stone on which you usually sit
that has forgotten to grow.
When I raise my hand to shake,
the door smiles.

The cat reminds me, "Hey, man, stop it."
I suddenly remember an unlit cigarette in my mouth.

I got married for two years, zero months, and twenty-nine days.
Choosing a night with no moon, you and I went to the swamp to
    make a fishing net.

Stuck in my pocket is a strange handwritten letter
in which there's a trace of sweat, or a lightning strike
from a thicket, or the sandy shore of the river's source.
So tonight I sleep with a picture,
only just
                        one.

Linh Dinh (1963–)

Born in Saigon, Linh Dinh came to the United States in 1975 and was educated at The University of the Arts in Philadelphia. He has published two story collections, *Fake House* and *Blood and Soap,* and the poetry collections *All Around What Empties Out* (2003), *American Tatts* (2005), *Borderless Bodies* (2005), and *Jam Alerts* (2007). A novel, *Love like Hate,* is forthcoming. He is editor and co-translator of the anthology *Night, Again: Contemporary Fiction from Vietnam* and the poetry collection *Three Vietnamese Poets.* An admirer of Céline and Kafka, he considers himself "a poet of the body," but he also identifies with the formal gamesmanship of Borges. Poet and critic Susan Schultz has identified in his writings the element of "empathy as disgust (or is it the other way around?)" or "better put: empathy after disgust." In a review of Linh Dinh's fiction, Thuy Dinh writes that his title "Fake House" can also mean "Nha Nguy" in Vietnamese. In addition to house, "Nha" refers to home or country. In addition to fake, "Nguy" can mean "puppet," with its implications of false or puppet government. Because he doesn't feel entirely comfortable in his first language, Vietnamese, nor the acquired language of English (he writes in both), Linh Dinh speaks of himself as a "hyper-conscious writer." In examining "objectivist" use of images, Susan Schultz writes, "His images are always precise, like Reznikoff's, but they are not clean; there is always interference in a Dinh poem." Interference is of course a feature of consciousness, which in a heightened state reaches surrealist fecundity and exactitude.

BORDERLESS BODY

Before, I was a miserly person, dried up, stiff,
Stuck completely wrung, stuttering, fanatical,

But this morning, my skin felt unusually cool and conscious.
My body tingled. Suddenly I could understand and speak

2,000 languages. My soul blossomed, my breasts budded.
I peeled back my foreskin to scrape clean all of my obsolete

And labored presumptions. My teeth, the gaps in between
My teeth and my breath felt unusually fresh and clean.

I could see very far away. I could sympathize with each
Strand of hair stranded on the skin of each person.

Shuddering, I ejaculated for the first time in my life, into life.
I became aware of my miraculous vagina and anus.

Finally, I had been allowed to spread out, to blend into
All humans, animals and things. I just wanted to leap up

To kiss everyone right away. I just wanted to service
And suck everyone right away. I also wanted to be sucked

By everyone on this earth. I was willing to forgive
And apologize to each toe joint on each person.

Naked, I walk through Saigon as the first Vietnamese.

DON'T

According to a theory, the first word
Ever uttered was perhaps "don't."
Managing an unruly horde of kids,
The cave mother had to "don't" nonstop.
Don't [put that thing in your mouth]!
Don't [climb up that branch]!
Don't [wake your father up]!

150,000 years ago, the main purpose of language
Was to prohibit. In many places on earth, now,
The main purpose of language is still to prohibit.

You know how it is: it is late afternoon and you suddenly find yourself in the dreadful town of Signa, standing in a bright café with a cold one in your hand? Well, I am leaning against the bar holding a Peroni, my fourth or fifth, and surrounding me are middle-aged men in rumpled suits downing shots of *amaro*. The potato chips and peanuts are actually free. A pensive ten-year-old girl pauses in front of the cash register, postponing for a few seconds the precious purchase of a bar of Emozioni. But my attention, for the last two hours or so, has been diverted from all these folks to a woman sitting alone at a table. Conventionally dressed but in a pair of men's shoes, sitting alone at a table, she is drawing a series of self-portraits with a set of colored pencils. Multiplied by an infinity of angles, the human face is really a kaleidoscope, an infinity of faces, and it is truly a miracle we can recognize each other (or ourselves) at all. But this woman has committed to memory all the essentials of her own physiognomy, and can conjure up, time and again, her own basic likeness without resorting to a mirror. She draws grimly yet fanatically, with an angry concentration that erases everything from the world but a tragic nostalgia for her own face. The café is transformed into a private monastery cell, with the rest of us reduced to dim ghosts blurring the edges of her bright vision. Each portrait is made to look different from the others: one depicts her as she appeared just this morning, at sunrise, emerging from a dream-racked sleep; another depicts her in the throes of love, just last night or maybe more than a decade ago; another depicts her as an anonymous child of three; and yet another depicts her as a marmoreal corpse, lying in a garlanded and perfumed coffin, awaiting our final nods of respect.

K-9 DOGS

I'm sitting in a room with K-9 dogs.
One more ugly person in the world.
A mother has claimed she's not my queen.

The lobe of an ear costs ten-weeks' paychecks.
Two hippies and a faggot.
Useless questions eloquently posed.

A posse cannot but be what it seems.
One more pair of jeans with a hole in it.
An extension cord hanging from the ceiling.

A cellist stoops to take a bow.
His cropped skull has no scars to mar it.
Although his nose has just been punched.

I drank two beers and ate a pretzel.
Two Mozarts flank me on both sides.
Across the room is the Dalai Lama.

His immaculate head has been spit-shined.
How many more times must I say this.
Nowhere but here can it matter.

EATING AND FEEDING

Always starving, he suckled his wife.
Famished, she sucked her husband.

For appetizers, he nibbled her fingers and toes,
While she gnawed on his shanks and thighs.

Becoming intimate with each other's meat,
They marinated each other's meat, to stew,
Deep fry or roast, or they ate each other raw.

Even with exposed bones, tendons and flesh,
They still had each other, two intact heads

To smile at each other each sunrise.

A REACTIONARY TALE

I was a caring husband. I bought socks for my family.

My swarthy wife liked to wear these thick woolen socks that came up to her milky thighs.

I had a lover also. People could see me walking around each evening carrying a walking stick.

My most vivid memory, looking back, is of a pink froth bubbling out of my infant's mouth.

Not everything was going so well: one morning, malnourished soldiers marched down our tiny street, bringing good news.

When good news arrives by mail, the cuckoo sang, tear up the envelope. When good news arrives by e-mail, destroy the computer.

When an old friend came by to reclaim an old wound, I said to my oldest son: Go dump daddy's ammo boxes into the fragrant river.

To reduce drag, some of my neighbors were diving headfirst into a shallow lake.

We were rich and then we were poor. A small dog or maybe a cat now pulls our family wagon.

AFTER ZIGZAGGING

After zigzagging across an open field,
How did I ever learn so many words
I can't pronounce?

After hiding under so many beds,
How did I ever learn to paraphrase
My nose? Eyes? Boils? Scar distribution?

And who was it that taught me to rearrange my teeth?

In darkness, in privacy, I squat, tabulating
My special stink. My breath
Has been mistranslated. And yet,
I can still kiss its veneer, stroke its vinyl.

And yet, just this morning,
As I crossed a seven-span bridge, as I
Crossed a twelve-span bridge, going both ways,
As I crossed and recrossed a hundred-span bridge,
A flock of dun-colored pigeons serenaded me.

Now I will pretend to lug my thin rump homeward.
A Kafka, a Jew, a stowaway monkey: "Hello!"
Freeze dried, flash frozen.

THE MOST BEAUTIFUL WORD

I think "vesicle" is the most beautiful word in the English language. He was lying face down, his shirt burnt off, back steaming. I myself was bleeding. There was a harvest of vesicles on his back. His body wept. "Yaw" may be the ugliest. Don't say, "The bullet yawed inside the body." Say, "The bullet danced inside the body." Say, "The bullet tumbled forward and upward." Light slanted down. All the lesser muscles in my face twitched. I flipped my man over gently, like an impatient lover, careful not to fracture his C-spine. Dominoes clanked under crusty skin: Clack! Clack! A collapsed face stared up. There was a pink spray in the air, then a brief rainbow. The mandible was stitched with blue threads to the soul. I extracted a tooth from the tongue. He had swallowed the rest.

Hoa Nguyen (1967–)

Hoa Nguyen was born in a small town near Saigon. Her father, a US soldier whose unit was shipped out of the area, never lived with the family; her stepfather, also a US soldier, arranged for Hoa Nguyen and her mother to live with him in the Washington, DC area, where she attended public school and was given the school name of "Millie." After attending New College of California at the suggestion of Robert Grenier, where she studied with Tom Clark, Gloria Frym, and David Meltzer, she moved to Austin, Texas, in 1997, where she lives today. With her husband, the poet Dale Smith, she edits the literary magazine and book imprint *Skanky Possum* and curates a monthly reading series. Her first full-length collection of poems, *Your Ancient See Through*, with line drawings by Philip Trussell, was published by Subpress in 2002. Among her other chapbooks is *Red Juice* (Effing Press, 2005).

EURASIACAN

No mother in body   no
body   when on the phone
meatballs simmering in sauce

Maybe my baby
whitens me
Turtles and blue eyes

"Pet" turtles discarded
in the pond
crusty deformed shells

Ground deer
meatballs mixed
in my mutt hands

Ma=horse
Ma=rice seedling
Ma=graveyard
Ma=mother

My boy walks
arms out   pointing
at the window

Yes, you saw a lizard
there once   Yes you rode
a dolphin   and a seal

THE GODDESS GAVE ME ROSES

The goddess gave me roses   several
loose blooms   the way my cervix flowered
and let the baby out

    We drink tea
a rose tied to her waist   the rose
is a baby and flames regard
the cracked pottery where women's things
are   is culture   domestic

Dale says   according to Sauer
that men only later and then "reluctantly"
took up domestic ways   weaving
clay works   the cooking arts   language

Women as masters & teachers

The goddess came as a stinkbug
on the edge of her tea cup
6 black legs edged in dusty red
Back shaped like a shield
with a faint *x* topped by a *y*

Grackles eat the cat food

LACY LIGHT

for D., K., and Way

Lacy light through new curtains
    curtains Mary made

and seem recent like lamp oil
burning on my shoulder

It's chaos & love   Big
           Old

Being literal about banjos
stuck to kneecaps

Crack up   say mangos

O Susannah   o don't you cry

It's a mango on my knee

Nhat Le (1968–)

Nhat Le was born in Quang Binh Province; grew up in Hue, where she took a degree in Russian from Hue Pedagogic University; and now lives in Ho Chi Minh City as a journalist on a daily newspaper. Nhat Le, who is not a member of the Vietnamese Writers Association, is seen as a "new face" whose work reveals not only her own life but also her generation as a whole. Her poetry expresses the struggles of a sensitive heart forced to come to terms with modern life despite an awareness of potential pitfalls in Vietnam's entry into the free enterprise system. Her representation of the individual in society reflects the thinking of her generation, but her means of expression is bolder and more assertive than that of any previous literary figure. That she both realizes her loneliness and strives to control it makes her a true poet. While Nhat Le's production has been modest, the poems she has produced are the richest of her generation.

UNTITLED [YESTERDAY]

Yesterday, I realized that some people were secretly staring
    into my soul
They discovered a few disloyalties—betrayals
I just laughed in their faces
I can't imagine what they will do with my dark thoughts
Maybe they will shoot me with a police whistle
or finger their thoughts to make them nastier
While I'm waiting, maybe they will crush me
with their powdery comments
and acupuncture faces
Then they leave
making me so confused
I follow them with questions
They say
they can read me just the way I am
Day by day we become more familiar!

MYSELF

Everywhere I look is
black
Autumn takes off its bra for the sky to suck
its huge imagination
In the darkness, streets are overturned
Garbage dumps fly through the sky
People breathe a strange and fresh air
Deaf black houses are silently shocked
by each ticktock
Lying in darkness
I feel consoled
that my eyes are still embedded in
cubits of darkness, the most attractive color
for clothing, which I use to cover my face and furious body
The faint lines in my chaotic thought
and the feeling of being prevented from sharing an apartment
are completely nasty
The rippling black glances of my son this morning
when he looked at me meant: "Mom, please die!"
His four-year-old's hatred
makes me remember the freshness of loving,
the kind I haven't seen for a very long time
because everything is colored
and covered by foil
The blackness of spoiled fish
fried and yellowed in tomato juice
is an epicurean blackness
a memory to be shot and smashed
The ambition of blackness
makes me lose sleep unceasingly
Insensitivity

licks me
makes me smile and want to be at peace,
but it still crawls up my body and swallows my youth

In the end, I return to my room
needing a loss of memory
and the door is completely closed!

WHEN I'M 23

23 years old
I don't want anything explained to me
because I'm unreasonable about real life
The world of adults is like a honey jar
It seduces me
although I lack the ability
to love and deal with it

23
So many things are broken up
A huge world surrounds me
at the center of the crash zone

23
I dream of being a mother
but don't want to give up my fate for my child
and don't know how to chose
a father for him

23
I love to use strong, active verbs
and adjectives that can hang me up by my feet
but I can't understand
what's strong enough to hang upside down by

IF YOU KNOW HOW TO LOVE ME

Fireflies lie flat on a field
Their lives are buried in festivals
but now I just want to ask you
if you know how to love me. . . .

You are the only one who believes in perfect loving
It's so simple why I chose you
You don't have anything that's costly
including yesterday's pensiveness in late blinking

Now you're my prisoner
You think you know your life,
but not who makes you boil
in this moment I give you

You don't have to know much about me,
only what a wolf must know when its prey suddenly cries
kissing it to the soft moment of death
when it shivers

If you know how to love me
perhaps we should create something
before, closing our eyes forever,
death has to kiss our lips

THE FATHER

I hide my heart in an underground prison
clear all romantic dreams from my head
and return to accepting the shame
of being with my father

Daddy, you don't see my tearful heart
You don't see the many sunsets converging into a solid sadness
I walk silently through your old age
but you don't know that I'm crying for your youth!

Daddy, you have woven my life into a flower
but why, when my heart—a young woman's heart—
is weighed down by your loneliness and your faults?
A journeyer who carries his smiles only in search of his own joys

Don't be tired, daddy, when I'm here beside you and can still taste
    your hopelessness
I can't bear your life, but I can throw myself as silently as pebbles
onto the lake's surface—your shadow ragged with old teardrops . . .

AUTUMN

The autumn draws two white lines that cross on a window
Sadness digs gradually into me
before it sleeps in silence

I walk through myself like a stranger
Spend my whole life sleeping so I can't see
myself—
a self unrelated to me and nasty as a murder
or a wild dog licking its bloody past

Autumn keeps drawing its portrait of a coffin
used for burying my fear
or could it be that I'm the one
who died?

FREEDOM

I'm never able to move gently
on my own
Even when tiptoeing, it's easy to lose my balance
never thrusting my chest forward
like a wild-sad-pensive goat

I run again and again into a forest
where I float up and down numbly above myself
then give myself up as a prisoner
to the one who loves me

There's not enough time to have my own name, not even libertine
I'm freedom that is stabbed in the heart
Life in prison makes me realize I will always be standing outside
looking at the word *happy* engraved on a bright door
What I have
is a wasted life
Other lovers pity me
but don't have to beg for their heaven
They tell me some baloney
about freedom
But the feeling of freedom for me
is that of a volcano

UNTITLED [SUNLIGHT]

The compassionate pores
of evening sunlight contain my emotion
and make me feel that I have to go somewhere,
do something
to occupy my time.
I don't know.
These pores
signal the loneliness
and joylessness
I'm trying to save for myself,
to restore my soul
when I have nothing left.
I'll start as a wild, dangerous animal
or the foolishness of childhood.
When these pores
open to become raindrops,
I'm as swollen and tense as a dry meadow.
The evening is so hot
it turns my pores into vacuums,
and I suck in thunderstorms.
Someone makes me
yell, curse, smile, and silently think
I'm being replaced,
being emptied out. Then I roam a street where nobody knows me.
A dog approaches, wagging its tail—
one dog only!
I ask these moments to break open, please,
so I can slip inside.
I won't search for immortality

or lust after life
but simply breathe through my pores,
becoming wider and wider
under the sunlight. . . .

Truong Tran (1969–)

Born in Saigon, Truong Tran immigrated with his family in 1975 to the San Francisco Bay Area, where he still lives. He earned his undergraduate degree from the University of California at Santa Cruz and his MFA degree in creative writing from San Francisco State University. Published in numerous poetry magazines, including *ZYZZYVA, The American Voice, Crazyhorse,* and *Poetry East,* he has published three full-length poetry collections with Apogee Press: *placing the accents* (1999); *dust and conscience,* which won the Poetry Center Book Award in 2002; and *within the margin* (2004), a book-length poem that often contains a single line per page. Juan Felipe Herrera has described *within the margin* as the "ashes, margins, and dislocations made of—war, memory, childhoods, deaths." Lyn Hejinian writes, "Along with writers like Pamela Lu and Renee Gladman, Tran is advancing the interrelated questions of narration, historiography, and identity . . . . *dust and conscience* speaks of a cultural position that simultaneously and from the start resists both marginalization and assimilation."

RECIPE 5

the Vietnamese market on Sundays
sells *hột vịt lộn*
baby ducks days   from hatching

boiled   salted a delicacy
when eaten accurate   swift
straight from the shell

children are warned
ăn thì phải nhắm mắt lại—
when eating keep your eyes closed

SCARS

my father's body is a map
a record of his journey

he carries a bullet
lodged in his left thigh
there is a hollow where it entered
a protruding bump where it sleeps
the doctors say it will never awaken

it is the one souvenir he insists on keeping
mother has her own opinions
bố của con điên—your father is crazy

as a child
i wanted a scar just like my father's
bold and appalling   a mushroom explosion
that said i too was at war
instead i settled for a grain of rice
a scar so small look closely there
here between the eyes
a bit to the right
there on the bridge of my nose

father says i was too young to remember
it happened while i was sleeping
leaking roof the pounding rain
drop after drop after drop

PLACING THE ACCENTS

left undisturbed on the piano's mantel
ashes of incense in a cup of sand
ikebana flowers leaning towards morning
left to die on a converted shrine
a deserted home lived in only
by the presence of your portrait

...

lāo già—old man come sit down and drink some tea
I've brewed oolong your favorite
as a child I watched you unraveling
tea leaves still wet and warm
in your palm we found butterflies   frogs
an elephant with two ears   a trunk   a tail
imagine finding an elephant
in the belly of a tea pot

...

she left not long ago
with suitcase   car keys   a fold-up mattress
to act a stranger in a stranger's home
some white rice in a bowl
a few slivers of bitter melon
pickled and placed in a saucer of fish sauce
this is all that she will have
she says eating bitter is what she does best

...

it was the first real conversation
we had in months

hoa fuschias của bố
đã chết chửa?

not yet má
dying but not dead.
when are you coming . . .

shhhh . . .

...

she helped me write this poem
with eyeglasses tilted on the bridge of her nose
pen in hand as if holding a needle
she embroidered the accents onto this paper cloth
as you would have done with chisel   hammer
your voice demanding   *it's time you learn*

inception incipience debut dawn where would i begin if not at home

...

to preserve the bitterness he scattered his children in four direc-
tions sat back in his chair and proceeded to grow old he waited
until the time was right he paid them a visit when they went to kiss
their father he licked their skin he found the bitterness still clinging
to his tongue he tells his children i want to go home

...

approach it as you will but do so knowing that the line which con-
nects the perceptions to the perceived is crossed with the line of
the needs and necessities and there at the crossing are the casualties
fragments to stories some still struggling to find the beginnings

...

hers is a story all too familiar the story of those left behind father-
less forever searching in an existence where forever is finite this she
tells me is a necessity hers is the story of conflicting hair disowning
her in one culture or another the story of skin thickened by sun
and neglect years upon years hers is the story of possession a dog
tag is no substitute but it will have to do

...

that is his death we have returned to wade along these flooded
streets to eat of the fruits our tongues have forgotten making good
on the promise made between a father and a son the beginnings to
an end without singularity in such a time in such a place i think of
it as arriving at a context

...

my lady of the lake with your ebony smile in a past life you lived as my mother and i your son wandering from market to market town to town with the weight of dragon fruits on our shoulders you and i my lady of the lake we are not so different beyond this threshold of distance and time that an orange is orange from where i come from this my lady of the lake is but a minor discrepancy for beyond any threshold is the promise of home

...

i've located you to a letter in the alphabet do not think it wrong of me it is by no means a reduction of your being this is done only so that i may address you free of the inhibitions found in a name they are temporarily submerged if not discarded let's say that you are k and i am t removed from our context t met k in country v t fell in love with both k and v the sum of which is a language unrequited

...

she sits in her new car she listens to the cd she is reminded of home she is overwhelmed with sadness she is parked in her garage she is reminded of home

...

i walk these streets as if you were beside me walking step for step the distance of the lake on this given day no giant turtle has emerged from the waters nothing of the fable you've told has fruitioned only the comfort of a satisfying walk a game of badminton to settle the score then and only then would we part you to explore your place of birth and i to find a tranquil moment then and only then would I arrive at your mourning

...

that series of photos i saw on tv of the one man he was pointing a gun at the temple of another man had he not pulled the trigger in that instance of the third frame each decision not arrived at holds a reality of its own had there been no effect to document on film to frame and reframe had there been no cause to arrive at the word *war*

...

my father as the scholar instead of the soldier teaching his way towards an early retirement my mother says i would have been married in saigon settled with two children as for that man in the picture holding the gun where would he be now as it is decisions arrived at somewhere in southern california he owns a restaurant i've written a poem

...

it is not that i am forgetful or lazy i have written letters to each and every one of you but i choose not to send them for such an act means that the existence of home would then be confined to one or the other

...

the lanterns made to usher in the full moon an art form that dies with the father in a foreign land left intact is the slivering of bamboo images of the past shelved to collect dust waiting for rebirth into the familiar as in the shadow that steps into itself so that the child may emerge whole existing on his own terms

...

dear suzanne the world is nothing as we know it i am sitting in a café where stools of bamboo make for seats wind as if derived from liquid heat blows at me from all directions the music in the background is prewar french and the women who pass by this café window have mastered the art of riding sidesaddle dodging traffic as predictable as life so you i'm sure can understand it when i say that the world is nothing as i know it and yet i sit at this window as if i were there

...

yes the stories are at times overwhelming but would i stop listening the answer is no for without the stories there would be no history and without the history there would be no people where then would i be if not the acronym the oddity the visitor the native

Mộng-Lan (1970–)

Visual artist and writer Mộng-Lan came to the United States as a child after the fall of Saigon in 1975. Her first book of poems, *Song of the Cicadas,* won the Juniper Prize and was published by the University of Massachusetts Press in 2001. *Song of the Cicadas* subsequently won the Great Lakes Colleges Association's Prize for New Writers and was a finalist for the Norma Farber First Book Award from Poetry Society of America. Her poetry has been anthologized in the *Pushcart Prize Anthology XXIV, Best American Poetry of 2002,* and *Asian American Anthology: The Next Generation,* and published in journals such as *The Kenyon Review, Colorado Review,* and *New American Writing.* She received the Dean's MFA Fellowship from the University of Arizona, a Wallace E. Stegner Fellowship from Stanford University, and a Fulbright Grant to Vietnam. In conjunction with the National Endowment for the Arts, she was chosen by the Dallas Museum of Fine Arts to be their first Visual Artist and Poet in Residence in 2005. Mộng-Lan travels extensively but spends most of her time in Tokyo, where she is an adjunct assistant professor with the Asian Division of the University of Maryland University College.

THE TASTE

of a sonata   adrift

your blanket   the moon   the sun

through trees specks of pepper

night wobbles a drunkard

at the dialectical borders

something is happening in the world   explosions

firecrackers in the night sky

like the coral's patient act

you untangle yourself from the net

of a dream

love was something you invented

drawing your shadows on rock

LETTERS

She has become like her mother
        her insides blooming
   she calms the gusts of hands & feet
           heartbeats delicate as geranium buds

    he's the salve of her sleep
        writing her letters over eleven years
before the rats nibble on the
           the house reads the words of his delirium
    which keeps the beams from rotting
        the cracks from spreading paint from fading
          blanketing sun & moon   the mist
    grays the decade

  at times he shakes from malaria
        forehead feverish   ice in his bones
       salves of his
    disease she's eleven years away

her one eye
     observes the grapefruit rinds worming
         on the dirt
  a love letter seen askew
divides the days of mist
    the house too having read
        them is preserved

GROTTO

Vịnh Hạ Long (Bay of the Landing Dragon), Tonkin Gulf

1

The rower gaunt as his oar

lets us out conscious

of not getting his 5,000 đồng

he stands ankles in cool water

holding onto the state-owned boat

for support his skin the same color

as the mud my eyes follow

the morning tides ebbing

from the dock

(flash of residue

undulating) turquoise solid

as the mountains mold has blackened

the boat's belly

lapping at it

clear water runs over sky

grotto of swimming bats I do not swallow

the darkness rocks under my feet

are piranhas' mouths if I miss a step

stalagmite meeting stalactites coincidences

taking forever to form

2

the eclipse's purple cast

throws everyone

off balance

inside   she clutches onto the image

of her lover   in case she falls

her body   a black-and-white lily

against the gorge

of sky   this morning she ate nothing

but a banana to quell

her upset stomach

a well drips its musical water

in the back   rock kings play chess

a centuries-old tournament

neither wins

dusky unbirth of pre-memory

she forgets to bring a flashlight

to disarm the rocks   stalagmites

a line of prayer to hook

her thoughts

3

bats swallow my shadow
                    when the ocean swallows us
          from these pages   what will the sky speak
          of   the bat grottos?
                         twenty years   the ugliness
          forgotten

back to port: bone sky
          mist bleeds over the mountain ridges
                         over water   barges snailing

racket of diesel motors
          a huge stone head
                         imagining us
          two rocks   two cocks fighting
                    a vigilant rock dog stares in silence

          my hand on the horizon
                         of its tail the scaly sieve

TRAIL

PRELUDE

        this age our era i can correctly say this an era of exile
this satiny desert
on this trail of a thousand years there is us amidst misfits &
    assiduous trees

we have walked
over sand sick with evening of words spilling

        what is the remedy for momentum for mania a
    deciduous heart?
loitering now i speak of nothing no ideas just viet nam
    motherland inside us
      & between us the air   the arizona sun magnanimous
    accepting everything

an ear of deaths in a polaroid photo & the killing
this age of hyperawareness this time of blue moons
      of the year nineteen hundred ninety nine on the seventh day

            the ocean   the past we touch
              inside our skin a sterling wound

we who have walked alone will no longer
through woods red with evening of dreams spilling
growing old a california sequoia   green &
           sage as the saguaro branching

a crab crawls sideways into a polaroid photo tangled you loiter
& now you speak of nothing no ideas pushed into hole the fabric
mice-chewed

you have been going back & forth from the border of . . . what was it?
when upon seeing a person with alzheimer's on tv when a flippant
offer of someone buying you something when after a family dinner
in which the main conversation was having desires versus shutting
them off you wander into the streets eyes wet while you notice how
roseate the sky is how demure the heat is not its usual how you
should be enjoying such a night but nevertheless you go wherever
your blind feet take you places well acquainted see cars pass &
wonder if the headlights expose & wonder if any will stop

wild eyed
next to your border a different dialect spoken
                              in the corridor your fingers pressed
listening monk this laughing buddha belly & shoulders twitter
a gurgle of ears listening pressed to palm
                                        when the mood strikes

      strike!
                              when i begin
              & drown in salt
                    the Buddha's my own or Lao Tsze's in this mesmer
          following the folds in robe

a boy dies saving another from suicide
on the suicide isle are mists gargantuan in deceptions

        words spilled the throat a babe on motorcycle
        rolls into the street

3

      to accelerate time I walk from arizona to texas
   to new york to   viet nam
most content while making forgetting that night is night
     (rug   cat hair   crumb)
                 & day day   this life is
to be in process is an act
   of survival
       follow the ends its awakened curves

through sterile passages of supermarkets i walk & walk
         to contend with time then suddenly   lack
slowness   then speed   a velocity problem

               a silver butterfly heavy

                 inside this drift split

4

       "within 100 years of contact with
       western civilization, the
       amazon tribes become extinct"

news lurking
not even metalsmithing nor the even-marking tires
the soles of defunct shoes
a blandness narrative can't obliterate

world news worsens these days
                    & you are not in my em-
          brace

          the axis spinning is why we don't fall off haunting earth
i haunt the earth
                    looking
     for a phone   this machine which allows us to be a-
                                        part
          how many digits is the number
                    for consciousness   the total for God?

no one knows me wandering in this flesh
over the desert-feet soles of those i will never know
i am eager for the packed streets the embroiled pavements I
     wander in books finding myself in paths that lead nowhere

               but to designs in nature

i rove through strip malls grocery aisles of stuff cans &
cans of songs looking   loitering & don't buy except
     what i need

               (the everpresent Present the future   it is here)
                    a fault line the world grins
          & yet this hand full of epiphanies
                    minds that cannot escape nonchalance

5

(*Chiapas*)

faces bought
from a witch   doctor
carved stone of desolation
shrines to the past (it is here)

a high turn of sea of sun
                         & from this black jade survival

gone to the market fed there a life led there entrails
    bowls of bowels eaten
          meat meat & through stalls the tents striped with
             humor & flirtation

& men jerking off do you ever get sick of this?
                       They do it with a life's content
      of blossoms / ever the orange flowers drowning

see the spiders spinning   caterpillars
          sheets of blisters ricocheting off surf
                      aztec blood of zapatistas

6

not for the cantilever of arguments
nor the cumulus remarks
        the confused odor of tolerable American lives
nor the razor the vein nor the contrapuntal snare do i come

but for the desert ranging on a contact sheet the outbreak
    of pneumonia
                        awkwardness of grand pianos
nonchalant pursuers of the dream the content hackers

i dream of sand dunes flying ridges & sun I dream of wind
    blowing darkly usurping cultural designs   a
        liar in a tiger's den

in this city a blissful terror of invisible spires
cryptic skies talk less & less
                            with my mother's hand
                        i tether jade to the skin of books

shoring over names of friends who have left the last rite
i carve over faces on stone

                    ((disclose with a kayak in throat))

                            7

                what noises are harbored in these chained boats?
        sometimes these moments alone from wood pulp bleached
                                    these thoughts
            are belligerent
                old women
                            i will be incoherent with them

                        8

                            my neighbors push
                            shopping
                            carts
                            home

amazonians on bare feet wooden dollies adorning
their lips
women on new york streets high heeled & aching

dreams of arizona: there are abscesses
households trying to make ends meet

dryness & trails
in heat people come out at night like lizards
watch each other rodents slither
the gila monster ecstatic

drawbridges dams impermeable we have our historical conclusions
try to live one day

10

this soil of extremes
a throb of mice in walls
assiduous trees a moon-shaped sickle
a dossier of stillness
see this aerial view
a body of shimmering water copies the blazing desert
water & some moon

twisted orifices of mountains
passing clouds shape of trees
waiting to see you I write this song on the plains
on spent mountains

try to sleep but words float up
what do animals do when they're alone?
they claw themselves til the blood flows (animals
                                    we're fine in motion)

        this is what time does to you
                        & clouds pass their leaves

            a snowflake fissured on window
                        patterned below the scandent mountains
            they've had a million years to practice their lines

Vi Thuy Linh (1980–)

Vi Thuy Linh lives and works as a journalist in Hanoi. Although not a member of the Vietnamese Writers Association, she has published three poetry collections. Her work is representative of Vietnam's newest generation, which knows of bombing from movies and books rather than personal experience. Her poems are very up-to-date in their strong and sometimes sexual display of emotion. Showing no fear of public censure, Vi Thuy Linh's work displays the optimistic and adventurous attitudes of her generation.

LYING DOWN FOREVER WITH THE MEADOW

A cry to my friend Vuong Dinh Binh

A collapse brings you to another world.
It's a long life, a thousand-mile path to its last station.
We are late to see the last of it.
Your eyes appear behind the smoke of incense.
My eyes fade like an old praise house.

The home region is named "The Future of the Sea," but it has no
    future except for its end.
The "safe" life is unsafe.
The collapse made you disappear.
I'm alive.
Continuing to live,
Continuing to fall!
A meadow trail has gone to seed from overuse.
You lie in a coffin as in a red ship.
At five o'clock of a swollen evening,
Linh wades into mud holding you and almost falls into a dark grave.
Fish splash turgidly in the watery meadow.
The old church is tall and compassionate in the sky.
The green burial ground of people who died before you is safe and
    dry on the left side of the meadow.
When can you open your arms and be as dry as that crossing?
Three years of learning to speak for another life,
Three years of meadow water flowing in.
You drove me to watch a movie and arranged to meet me at a
    sunny location,
But suddenly you are gone in the spring.
It makes my eyes drill holes into life,
a movie continuously showing people being just people.

Now, here,
I rain early in the day of a day's life span.

Let's blow our four glasses up to the sky to scratch the furious sun,
Putting down people who are cloaked with human kindness and
    brazenly live,
My friend, my friend!
Slough off your body and become a curving kite.
In the flooded water meadow,
We clean you with our tears.
The young girl rice is unexpectedly green
Pressed into the wind, the hymn flares up!

THE LOVE SEASON

When the eyes suddenly speak
A million seeds of yellow *lipa* flowers blow far away.
You appear as a gentle evening
Covering me and also the world with tears.

Continuing to look for you along with my youth early every
    morning and on cold evenings,
Continuing to look for you including in my dreams when they
    become nightmares,
It makes me feel busy, and I work too much.
But in fact, I can think only about you.

My fingers are keys that turn in dreams.
My freezing fingers scratch ancient deserts.
I call your name to fill me with energy,
So that once again you can give me structure.

We have left our youth, one piece at a time, in the place where we
    feel lost,
And our imaginations rebuild the memory
Where the hopeless collapse and leave layers of sadness.
I myself adopt the new hope
That these words will sprout from under my skin,
These words will mix my blood with your blood,
Lusting for an opening in the curve of conjugal night.

One day was gone as you were leaving.
Many years have gone since you left.
Our lips become ocean waves.
We have slept alone for many years in the hallway of our desires.
We have tossed and turned, counting the nights.

We swallow our groans.
We spin in the night like hands on a compass, seeking our signal's
     direction.
We fasten together mysteriously and wildly.

On the day you arrive, the season of love arises,
Opened by fingers that are also keys.

HANOI WITHOUT YOU:
AFTERWORD

Paul Hoover

In March and April of 2003, I traveled to Hanoi, Hue, Hoi An, and Saigon for two weeks. Through the efforts of novelist Larry Heinemann and Chicago writer Tom Nawrocki, I met both with the powerful Writers Association, headed by Huu Thinh, and with the "outsiders" group organized by Hoàng Hung. The rivalry of the two groups was immediately apparent and to some degree finds its parallel in American literary politics of the "inside" and "outside." But the repercussions of difference are much sharper in Vietnam. In the 1980s, Hoàng Hung was imprisoned in the "Hanoi Hilton" and reeducation camps merely on suspicion of possessing a banned manuscript of the poet Hoàng Cam. Released during the period of *glasnost,* he returned to his work as a journalist and is now one of the leading poets and translators in the country. But he does not enjoy the benefits of membership in the Writers Association, which brings with it position, salary, and benefits.

The Writers Association could not have been more hospitable at our meeting in Hanoi. After the traditional tea service and introductions of all in the room, Huu Thinh asked me, as editor of the W. W. Norton anthology of the same title, to comment on the situation of "Postmodern American Poetry." The writers present were much interested in the intellectual and cultural issues pertaining to postmodernism. They thought it ironic that Marxism had influence over our literary theory. Three of the group, Nguyen Duy, Nguyen Quang Thieu, and Huu Thinh, had already been published by Wesleyan University Press and Curbstone Press. Association members had many questions about standard publishing practices including royalty, ownership, and licensing arrangements.

This anthology includes poetry written by poets of both the "inside" and "outside," but it feels a special responsibility to represent the work of poets of the Nhan Van period and since who have been forced to write in marginal circumstances. This is the first poetry anthology published in the United States to do so. Indeed, up to this time, Vietnamese poetry published in this country has been exclusively that of Writers Association members.

When Hoàng Hung visited the United States for the first time in May, 2003, he introduced me to Nguyen Do, who moved from Vietnam to Sacramento in the late 1990s. This translation project was Do's idea, and, with the exception of the Vietnamese-American poets (Linh Dinh, Truong Tran, Mộng-Lan, and Hoa Nguyen), he has selected all the poems for inclusion. My task has been to create from his versions the best possible poems in English. Some poems were captured on the first couple of drafts; others required several exchanges. From the beginning, it was clear that the human drama of the poem lay readily apparent beneath the mask of cultural difference. As soon as we explained terms like "young girl rice" (rice with a sweet milkiness from being grown in regions with severe weather), the poets' local metaphors became universal. As with the recent translations of Hölderlin I've done with Maxine Chernoff, I saw the necessity of reading both with and ahead of the text, in search of the poem's purpose, its ironies and counterpoints, and especially its emotional and intellectual logic.

Our selection captures the diversity and sophistication of Vietnamese poetry, from the highly innovative work of Dang Dinh Hung and others to the lyrical expression of its traditional culture. The honesty and directness of political expression in Vietnamese poetry is impressive and might serve as a lesson to those of us living through the current war in Iraq. Thanh Thao's "A Soldier Speaks of His Generation" gives a vivid portrait of the life of a soldier; Nguyen Duy's "Looking Home from Far Away" candidly assesses the moral condition of his country in the period to follow the American War. Both men are among Vietnam's most popular poets. Our translation of Thanh Thao's poems, *12 + 3*, will be published in Vietnam in a bilingual edition under sponsorship of the Writers Association.

Modernism provides a point of stress in all literatures, bringing self-consciousness, individualism, and intellectual and formal difficulty in resistance to the folk traditions of ease, accessibility, and enjoyment. Both the modernist and folk traditions are represented in this volume. Dang Dinh Hung writes in a postsymbolist, associational mode of free verse, yet he maintains the melancholy tone of Quan Ho folk songs. Hoàng Hung's poetry is informed by existentialism and the Beat movement, yet it relies on the melodic use of Quan Ho forms. The forcefulness and candor of Nhat Le's poetry may remind some readers of the confessional styles of Sylvia Plath and Sharon Olds. Candor and everyday life are also features of the poetry of Vi Thuy Linh, but the settings and textures are unmistakably Vietnamese: "My eyes fade like an old praise house." Throughout this volume, it's the *khuyen* bird crying, the seeds of the *lipa* flower blowing. It's noteworthy, therefore, that the only Vietnamese directly quoted in this book appears in the work of Truong Tran, who has lived in San Francisco since 1975.

Are the Vietnamese-American poets different from their Vietnamese counterparts in some important way? Both Linh Dinh and Hoàng Hung, one American, one Vietnamese, are attracted by "dark" tones approaching the grotesque and dreamlike. Such matters of tone have to do with proclivity, literary influence (Dinh admires Kakfa, Hung is drawn to Ginsberg), and experience of the world. Hung's years in prison undoubtedly darkened his life and his poetry, but poetry also helped save him. Lacking access to paper, he would exercise his mind by composing poems in his head and reciting them to himself.

In an essay, the poet Susan Schultz has commented on the uses of disgust in Linh Dinh's poetry including "empathy as disgust." Disgust is also married to amazement and can find its source in cultural difference. In Linh Dinh's poem "Academy of Fine

Arts," he expresses pride that, even when he is nude, his ass-hole is not exposed. This makes him superior to dogs. In such poems, Linh Dinh creates fables around the figure of an astonished immigrant, amazed at his physical and cultural difference from the "perfect" and self-satisfied natives around him. In "After Zigzagging," he writes, "How did I ever learn so many words / I can't pronounce?" The poetry of Hoa Nguyen, on the other hand, has a tone of openness and everydayness reminiscent of the New York School poets. There is no division in her poetry of self from world, but rather an astute deepening of the actual, especially in taking the mysterious and yet comfortable role of mother. Even her name, *Hoa* ("flower"), suggests openness. But naming is also where multiple identities begin, especially for a Eurasian child born in Vietnam:

Ma=horse
Ma=rice seedling
Ma=graveyard
Ma=mother

The poetry of Truong Tran combines experimental modernism with a desire to comment and reflect upon personal experience, including that of identity. In the poems here selected, the figure of a missing, agonized, and wraithlike father is heightened by the use of formal intermittence and, in "The Book of Beginnings," an absence of punctuation that introduces a postmodern tone of indeterminacy. The work of Mộng-Lan has the look and range of reference seen in Barbara Guest and Charles Olson, but it is not laden with experimental intention. Not to play the distinction too heavily, but in the innovative formal structures of Truong Tran and Mộng-Lan, lyricism and self-dramatization attend the process. Of the two poets, Mộng-Lan is more drawn to philosophical figures such as "night wobbles a drunkard / at the dialectical borders." Poetry and politics share the genius of border location, dividing us between one state and another, ultimately to the benefit of both.

Presenting the poets in chronological order allows the reader to witness aesthetic change in parallel with historical developments: the importance of the New Poetry movement influenced by French romanticism; the turn toward a Soviet-approved aesthetics by means of the expansive, perfomative poetry of Mayakovsky; the courage of the Nhan Van group in the 1950s, their political suppression, and their stirring post-1989 revival; the travails of Hoàng Hung and others during the Vietnam-American War, when foreign influences, especially the French existentialist model of spiritual exhaustion, seemed especially threatening; and the arrival of younger women poets like Nhat Le and Vi Thuy Linh in the post-1989 period, who feel free to express themselves personally, sexually, and existentially.

Like Chinese, from which it derives, Vietnamese consists of one-syllable words, which, along with the language's complicated use of accentuation, create an entirely different rhythm than the polysyllables of English. It's impossible, therefore, to replicate the cadences of a Vietnamese poem. One must rely on the cadences, rather, of thought and tone. Some poets here included make use of traditional forms, which can mean a given number of figures to the line, usually four or five. Thus, the first line (five figures) of "Viewing the Three Lakes" by Hsieh T'iao reads:

accumulated / water / reflect(s) / red / clouds

In English, the closest form we have is "counted verse," in which a given number of words, rather than syllables, appears in each line. May Swenson, Bob Perelman, and Louis Zukofsky, among others, have employed the form with success. Counted verse privileges the individual word. As each new word takes on weight, value, and context with its neighbors, the rest of the poem adjusts in tone, extension, compression, and color. It's not that each word is polished into a decorative smoothness but rather that it is suitable both in relation and in difference. Being more resolute, sentences lend themselves readily to statement and persuasion. Counted verse allows for a slower and more intuitive word rhythm, perhaps because of the tension between the arbitrariness and "necessity" of its word selection.

I would like to thank Nguyen Do for his friendship, collaborative spirit, and for the example of his own poetry. I would also like to thank Hoàng Hung and members of the Hanoi Writers Association, who made my visit to Vietnam such a pleasure, and Columbia College Chicago, which provided the funding. I'm grateful to be part of this freshening of Vietnamese poetry for the reader in English, who will see the wide-ranging themes and styles of poetry being practiced.

ACKNOWLEDGMENTS

Some poems in this anthology have been previously published in English in the following journals:

American Poetry Review:

Linh Dinh: "Self-Portraitist of Signa"

Cipher Journal:

Hoàng Hung: "A Peaceful Madman" and "Untitled [Where do the stairs lead us]"
Nguyen Do: "Morning" and "The Unlucky Days"
Nhat Le: "When I'm 23" and "If You Knew How to Love Me"
Thanh Thao: "To Suddenly Remember" and "A Soldier Speaks of His Generation"

New American Writing v. 23:

Dang Dinh Hung: "The New Horizon I"
Van Cao: "Three Variations at Sixty-Five Years Old"
Hoàng Hung: "A Man Returning Home," "Black Dog, Black Night," and "The Madwoman"
Thanh Thao: "March 12" "To Suddenly Remember" and "A Soldier Speaks of His Generation"
Nguyen Do: "A Symphony of Friendship," "The Unlucky Days," and "Mission"
Nhat Le: "Myself" and "When I'm 23"

Nguyen Quang Thieu: "The Spirits of Cows"
Vi Thuy Linh: "Lying Down Forever with the Meadow"
Nguyen Duy: "Looking Home from Far Away"

Parthenon West Review v. 3:

Hoàng Hung: "A Dog of Stone," "Fever," "The Night of Crossing
the Pass," "A Peaceful Madman," "A Rainy Night," "A Poem
Belonging to M," and "Untitled [Where do the stairs lead us]"
Xuan Quynh: "Love Poem in Late Autumn" and "A Lullaby"

**Some poems in this anthology previously appeared in English
in book form, and the editors are grateful for permission to use
them:**

"the book of beginnings" in *dust and conscience* (Berkeley, CA: Apogee Press 2002). Copyright © 2002 by Truong Tran. Reprinted with the permission of Apogee Press.

"Grotto," "Letters," and "the taste" in *Song of Cicadas* (Amherst, MA: University of Massachusetts Press 2001). Copyright © 2001 by Mộng-Lan. Reprinted with the permission of University of Massachusetts Press.

"Trail" from *Why Is The Edge Always Windy?* by Mộng-Lan, published by Tupelo Press. Copyright 2005 by Mộng-Lan. All rights reserved. Reproduced by permission of Tupelo Press.

The editors wish to express their appreciation to the following individuals and organizations:

Nguyen Do

I am thankful for the extraordinary hard work and friendship of my companion, Paul Hoover, and his wife, Maxine Chernoff, co-editors of *New American Writing*. My sincere thanks to professors Thomas Brett, Dianne Heimer, and Dagne Tedla of Sacramento City College, who helped me not only to increase my proficiency in English but also sometimes to decrease my loneliness as a "reform camp" student of English as a second language. I extend special thanks to editorial cartoonist Rex Babin and journalists Bob Sylva and Allen Pierleoni of *The Sacramento Bee*, who have encouraged me throughout this project.

Finally, I would like to thank my friends Thanh Thao, Hoàng Hung, and Nhat Le, who have long been arm in arm with me not only in our works but also in our fates, through all the ups and downs; and, of course, as always, I thank my mother Phan Thi Quy, my father Nguyen Xuan Bong, my lovely daughter Nguyen

Au Huong, my wonderful sister Nguyen Thu Hang, and my lovely friends Hoàng Ngoc and Helen Nguyen, who are the most important people in my life.

Paul Hoover

I am thankful to my former colleagues, Tom Nawrocki and Dominic Pacyga of Columbia College Chicago, for including me in a junket to Vietnam in the spring of 2003. During our visit to Hanoi, I met the poet Hoàng Hung and was drawn closer to the world of Vietnamese letters. On his first trip to the United States the following summer, Hoàng Hung introduced me to Nguyen Do, which led to our fruitful relationship as editors and translators. My thanks to Huu Thinh, head of the national Vietnamese Writers Association, for inviting me to speak to members of the association at their Hanoi offices, followed by a splendid banquet and traditional music from some of the country's leading performers. I am grateful to Larry Heinemann, who made the Writers Association visit possible, and to Nguyen Duy for serving as our host while in Ho Chi Minh City. Thanks to Thai Ba Tan, Vietnam's leading translator of Shakespeare, for serving as translator at the Writers Association meeting, after two other translators found the literary discussion to be too difficult.

I would like especially to thank Nguyen Do for inviting me to join him in this important translation project. I am thankful also for his friendship.

Our thanks to everyone at Milkweed Editions. We are especially grateful to Daniel Slager, Editor in Chief, for his interest in the project and helpful evaluation of the text.

As always, I would like to thank Maxine Chernoff and our children Koren, Philip, and Julian for their love and support.

NOTES

Huu Loan

"The Purple Color of Sim Flowers"

"Green" is an idiom for a young Vietnamese person's black hair. "Your hair is still green" means "You are still young."

In rural Vietnam it's traditional for the groom's family to give the bride new clothing; her not requesting a new shirt suggests that she is modest and understands the family's limited means.

The yellow grass at the poem's end suggests aging and death.

Te Hanh

"Hanoi Without You" was written in 1980.

"The Old Garden" was written in 1957.

Longan, also known as "Dragon's Eye," is a greenish-brown fruit. In Vietnam, it called *nhan* or *nhan long*.

"Missing My Home River" was written in 1957.

From 1954 to 1975, Vietnam was divided into two parts, South and North, by the seventeenth parallel.

Van Cao

"Sometimes" was written in 1963.

"Empty" was written on September 1, 1958.

"A Beer Joint" was written in 1967.

"The Door" was written in 1960.

"Nightly Restaurant" was written in 1967.

> *Ruou* is Vietnamese vodka made from rice or corn.

"Three Variations at Sixty-Five Years Old" was written in September 1988.

"Five Unreal Mornings" was written in 1960.

> *Khuyen* is a pretty Vietnamese bird similar to a golden-crowned kingbird that sings at the approach of spring.

Hoàng Cam

"I Live in Quan Ho Circle"

> "Leaning on a corner post" refers to an element of a traditional Vietnamese country house.

> Quan Ho Circle is a very popular group of Vietnamese traditional singers and their musicians who perform annually at the beginning of spring.

> "Couples in love would immediately gather and sift rice straws to make their bed mats" refers to the old practice in Vietnamese villages of using rice straw to make mattresses.

> "The *betel* and *areca* with grilled pink rice hadn't yet matched" means that things required of the engagement ceremony hadn't enough time "sitting" together before the wedding ceremony's traditional exploding of firecrackers in front of the bridegroom's house. Also, *betel* in the shape of phoenix wings would have been left over from the wedding.

"The Dieu Bong Leaf"

> Because the young woman doesn't know what she really wants, she creates an imaginary object of desire instead, the *Dieu Bong* Leaf.

Tran Dan

"A Man Made of Flesh"

Table de nuit refers to a small table in a bathroom for use at night.

Sputnik was the name of Russian space satellites.

In the next to last line, *kilos* refers to kilometers.

Nguyen Khoa Diem

"The Huong Giang Evening"

Huong Giang is a river in the city of Hue, at the center of Vietnam.

"A Country Place" was written in March 1985.

Xuan Quynh

"Love Poem in Late Autumn"

The *Heo May* wind blows northeast and appears only in late fall.

Hoàng Hung

"The Madwoman" was written in Hai Phong.

"A Peaceful Madman" was written in Hai Phong in the 1960s.

"A Rainy Night" was written in Ho Chi Minh City, on June 6, 1993.

"A Man Returning Home"

That refers to prison, but is simply the emphasized word in English, "that."

"America"

> *Ram* is the August 15 folklore holiday of the lunar year when the moon is perfectly round and bright.

"Untitled [Where do the stairs lead us]"

> *Bim* is a Vietnamese flower.

"Untitled [The faint, dark hallways]"

> *Co may* is a grass that grows in Vietnam.

"The Smell of Rain or A Poem Belonging to M" was written on June 25, 1992.

Tran Vu Mai

"The Grassy Banks of Hong River" was written in Hanoi in March 1971.

> The Hong River runs through Hanoi.

> The "South Pole" was an idiom used by soldiers sent to South Vietnam during the war with the United States.

Y Nhi

"A Woman Knitting" was written in January 1984.

"Song Lyric"

> *Khuyen* is a Vietnamese bird similar to the golden-crowned kingbird that sings at the approach of spring.

Thanh Thao

"To Suddenly Remember"

> In Vietnam, the word for "rainbow" also refers to an honor or glorious achievement.

"Wave Oscillation" was written in 1988.

"And You Wake Me Up, Ginsberg . . ." was written in 1998.

"This Is Usual" was written in 2004.

"A Journey" was written in 1994.

"The Goal" was written in 1988.

> *Truong Son* is the longest mountain range in Vietnam,
> running from north to south; along with the Ho Chi Minh
> Trail, it serves as the border between Laos and Vietnam.

"If I Knew" was written in 1998.

"A Soldier Speaks of His Generation" was written in 1973.

> This poem was very controversial in Vietnam after it was
> published in Hanoi's largest literary review, *Van Nghe,*
> and was prohibited by the government until 1988, when
> Vietnam reconstructed its economy and politics.

> *Giang* is a wild vegetable, sour to the taste, which North
> Vietnamese soldiers used in soup.

> *Dau* is a kind of tree commonly found in the forests of
> southwest Vietnam.

> *Thap Muoi* is a swamp where one of the largest North
> Vietnamese army camps was located.

> *Quoc* is a nocturnal bird that sings "*quoc, quoc, quoc*"; it
> also means "country."

> *Dien Dien* is a wildflower.

> *Bang Lang, My Long* is the name of a trail in *Thap Muoi* swamp.

> *Bang Lang,* the canal, is so named because it is lined with
> Bang Lang trees.

> *Tram and Binh Bat* are trees that can be found in *Thap Muoi*
> swamp.

> *Chuong* is a kind of Southwest wind.

Nguyen Duy

"Sitting in Sadness, Missing My Mother . . ."

Hue is a Vietnamese lily used in ceremonial offerings.

Yem is a special old-fashioned Vietnamese bra worn by the wealthy.

Quai thao is a conical hat with a silk chin strap.

Me is a conical hat for the poor.

Ram is the night of August 15, in the lunar year.

An areca-sheath fan is a fan made from the bark of the areca tree.

Thang Bom is a popular humorous folk song.

"Do Len" was written in the poet's grandmother's home in September 1983.

Do Len: All proper words are places in Thanh Hoa province, central North Vietnam, before 1975.

Van is a ritual Vietnamese song.

Dong is a kind of yam.

"Looking Home from Far Away" was written in Moscow, in May 1988.

"We are only ourselves, but we are passionate" is from a poem by Che Lan Vien, written at the time of the Vietnam-American War.

"When the paper tears, people still save its edge" is a traditional Vietnamese proverb.

"Blind eyes catch the goat" is part of a children's game of run and catch.

There is no such thing as a "cursing pill" in Vietnam. The term is used for satirical purpose.

The poem's final line is taken from a traditional folk poem.

Nguyen Quang Thieu

"The Spirits of Cows

Many villages in Vietnam are Christian, usually Roman Catholic—two million people or more. In this poem, it is the Eastern Church of Christ.

Nguyen Do

"Headache" was written in Ho Chi Minh City, on May 13, 1993.

"Memory of a Day" was written in Ho Chi Minh City in 1994.

"For My Lovely Au" was written in Sacramento in 2000.

Young girl rice is raised in the harsh conditions of the highlands in central Vietnam, where the strong wind from Laos creates a tender and moist grain.

"Mission" was written in Ho Chi Minh City, on September 13, 1995.

"Untitled [feeling extremely sad]" was written in Ho Chi Minh City, on September 18, 1991.

"The Unlucky Days" was written in Ho Chi Minh City, on March 25, 1993.

"Theme I" was written in Ho Chi Minh City, on October 31, 1996.

"A Lyric Song for Ngoc" was written in Sacramento between 2000 and 2005.

The sound "*au o*" occurs at the beginning of every Vietnamese lullaby.

"Silliness" was written in Sai Gon on April 18, 1994.

Nhat Le

"The Father" was written in 2004.

"Autumn" was written in 2004.

"Freedom" was written in 2004.

"Untitled [Sunlight]" was written in 2003.

Vi Thuy Linh

"Lying Down Forever with the Meadow" was written on September 19, 2000.

"The Love Season" was written on September 21, 2003.

Paul Hoover

Hanoi Without You: Afterword

Susan Schultz. "Most Beautiful Words: Linh Dinh's Poetics of Disgust." *Jacket* volume 27, April 2005.

Wai-Lim Yip. *Chinese Poetry: An Anthology of Modern Modes and Genres* (Duke University Press, 1997) pp 158.

Nguyen Do was born in Ha Tinh province in 1959 and moved to Hanoi as a youth. A poet, journalist, and translator, for a long time he lived in Ho Chi Minh City, where he worked as an editor and reporter for a literary review and many other newspapers and magazines before moving to the United States to study English. His poetry collections are *The Fish Wharf and The Autumn Evening* (1988, in collaboration with Thanh Thao) and *The Empty Space* (1991). While living in Vietnam, he wrote many articles criticizing the government and legal system. As a result, for eight years nothing he wrote could be published under his name. To make a living, he did sports and arts reporting under a dozen different pseudonyms. He is not a member of the Vietnamese Writers Association.

Paul Hoover was born in Harrisonburg, Virginia, in 1946. He is the author of eleven books of poetry including the *Edge and Fold* (Apogee Press, 2006) and *Poems in Spanish* (Omnidawn, 2005), which was nominated for the Bay Area Book Award in poetry.

With Maxine Chernoff, he has translated *Selected Poems of Friedrich Hölderlin* and, with Nguyen Do, "Beyond the Court Gate: The Selected Poems of Nguyen Trai."

He is also editor of the anthology *Postmodern American Poetry* (W. W. Norton, 1994) and, with Maxine Chernoff, the annual literary magazine *New American Writing*. His collection of literary essays, *Fables of Representation,* was published by University of Michigan Press in 2004.

He has received the Jerome J. Shestack Award for the best poems to appear in *American Poetry Review* in 2002. Author of the novel, *Saigon, Illinois* (Vintage Contemporaries, 1988), he is currently Professor of Creative Writing at San Francisco State University.

MORE POETRY IN TRANSLATION
FROM MILKWEED EDITIONS

To order books or for more information, contact Milkweed at
(800) 520-6455
or visit our Web site (www.milkweed.org).

Amen
Yehuda Amichai
Translated from the Hebrew by Ted Hughes

Astonishing World:
The Selected Poems of Ángel González 1956–1986
Translated from the Spanish by Steven Ford Brown
and Gutierrez Revuelta

The Art of Writing:
Lu Chi's Wen Fu
Translated from the Chinese by Sam Hamill

The House in the Sand
Pablo Neruda
Translated by Dennis Maloney and Clark Zlotchew

Trusting Your Life To Water and and Eternity:
Twenty Poems of Olav H. Hauge
Chosen and Translated by Robert Bly

Milkweed Editions

Founded in 1979, Milkweed Editions is one of the largest independent, nonprofit literary publishers in the United States. Milkweed publishes with the intention of making a humane impact on society, in the belief that good writing can transform the human heart and spirit. Within this mission, Milkweed publishes in four areas: fiction, nonfiction, poetry, and children's literature for middle-grade readers.

Join Us

Milkweed depends on the generosity of foundations and individuals like you, in addition to the sales of its books. In an increasingly consolidated and bottom-line-driven publishing world, your support allows us to select and publish books on the basis of their literary quality and the depth of their message. Please visit our Web site (www.milkweed.org) or contact us at (800) 520-6455 to learn more about our donor program.

Interior design by Wendy Holdman
Typeset in Minion Pro
by BookMobile Design & Publishing Services
Printed on acid-free Rolland
(100 percent postconsumer waste) paper
by Friesens Corporation